A River Runs Backward

FLAVORS & REFLECTIONS OF FLORIDA'S FIRST COAST

D1370814

> Tour the hometown river and beach
> communities of Jacksonville and
> Northeast Florida at the mouth of the
> St. Johns River, one of only two rivers
> flowing north in this hemisphere. *A
> River Runs Backward* is a collection of
> regional recipes, area history and
> family memories reflecting a neighbor-
> hood life-style of southern hospitality
> and outdoor living.

THE JUNIOR LEAGUE OF JACKSONVILLE, FLORIDA

A River Runs Backward

may be ordered through the Junior League of Jacksonville
at the following address.

Junior League of Jacksonville Headquarters
Cookbook Office
2165 Park St.
Jacksonville, FL 32204

(904) 387-9927

Printed in the USA by

WIMMER
The Wimmer Companies, Inc.
Memphis

ISBN 0-9609338-1-6

Table of Contents

*A*cknowledgments

*C*ookbook *C*ommittee

Kim Skinner, chairman
Kay Henderson, co-chairman
Wendy Morrow, editor
Kathy Magee, desserts
Dori Meadow, side dishes
Dawn Hudson, entrees
Laurie Yant, soups and
  sandwiches
J. J. Howell, breads
Linda O'Steen, salads
Julie Schulte, appetizers
Suzanne Holley, entertaining
Susie Morrow, entertaining

Henny Schoonover,
  entertaining
Debby Shaw, entertaining/
  sustainer adviser
Lee Shepherd, art director
Janis Bean, marketing
Tracy Tomlinson,
  marketing
Beth Hune, public relations
Sandra Lang, special events
Jill Barden, assistant editor
Debra Yale, historian

*Special thanks to the following people
who graciously gave of their time and expertise to
make this book a reality.*

Bill Blong, Blong Florist Inc.
Micheline Chelette, The Cookbook Center
Donna Hall
Susan F. Crosby, Words' Worth Publishing
Kathryn Abbruzzese
Catherine Damron-Food Stylist
Eileen Sabourin, The Cookbook Center
Stuart Findlay, food photography
Trevor Green
McElwee and McElwee and Marcy Appelbaum,
background photography
Wayne Wood
Rudy York, Rudy York Designs

A River Runs Backward

Our city, Jacksonville, is as accommodating and bountiful as the St. Johns River which meanders gracefully and steadily through it. Seemingly backward, the river, flowing from south to north, provides a dramatic setting for the downtown skyline, riverside restaurants and stately homes hovering its shores, reflecting the shades of times past and the twinkling lights of progress. The historical homes of Avondale, San Marco and Ortega, the quaint antique shops and inviting boulevards lend a feeling of rich family heritage that flows deeply through the city.

But, the river is not alone in its natural beauty and impact upon the area. Directly to the north is the fishing village of Fernandina. Its restored main street reflects a life tied to the sea.

Other neighborhoods defined by the vast Atlantic Ocean and the teaming Intracoastal Waterway offer a colorful and casual life-style. From the old beachfront homes of Atlantic Beach to the Tournament Players Club at Sawgrass,

Jacksonville Ferry 1897-1904
Photograph is from collections at The Jacksonville Historical Society Archives.

The 1858 Mayport Lighthouse and keepers residence in 1900.
Photograph is from collections at The Beaches Area Historical Society Archives.

residents and visitors alike play in the surf and relax under the beach's glow.

Southernmost Mandarin and Orange Park communities have histories as flavorful as the citrus for which they were named. From the times of the Timucuan Indians and the Spanish missions, the Civil War and Harriet Beecher Stowe to the modern bustle of growth, the people of these areas are proud of their legacy.

North of downtown, Springfield boasts some of the richest pockets of pre-1920's housing. This neighborhood is tightly knit by a commitment to preserve and restore its landmark treasures.

This is our city, host to many unique neighborhoods all sharing gracious living and a zest for life. Jacksonville offers a variety of entertaining events from our annual jazz festival to the symphony orchestra, from dinner theater to riverboat dancing, from grade school softball to Jaguar football, from cane pole fishing to the deep sea hunt. With the variety of life-styles and pastimes available to its residents, Jacksonville abounds with good times and creative entertaining.

The Junior League of Jacksonville reflects the warmth and character of these neighborhoods with each member contributing her own special blend of voluntarism and concern for the region. The League is committed to a lifelong participation in community affairs.

Formed in 1923, its charitable purpose has remained constant while its specific undertakings have met the challenges of each generation. Recently, volunteers have focused on children's issues, teen pregnancy, and literacy. One project, the Family Visitation Center, developed in conjunction with HRS and the Children's Home Society, provides a homelike atmosphere for parents and other relatives to have supervised visits with their children in foster care. With each endeavor the League. strives to encourage and celebrate a healthy community

We are proud to present this unique and delicious collection of recipes to share with all those who enjoy a passion for cooking, tempting aromas and memorable parties. Please allow our river of recipes to flow back toward you.

Residence of Wellington Wilson Cummer (Fisk and Riverside)
Photograph is from collections at Riverside Avondale Preservation Archives.

Our River Runs Backward, however, our desserts sail forward. In keeping with this theme, the memory below was submitted.

"My great-grandfather, Basil Hampton, named for two Civil War generals, was lovingly called "B.H." or "Bone-Head." His philosophy was somewhat backward. He'd say, "You never know when the good Lord will call you home, so Eat Dessert First!"

Some other notes which may help you as you cook are listed below.

- All flour listed in recipes is unbleached flour unless otherwise noted.

- Recipes marked with a palm tree are low in fat.

- Vanilla refers to vanilla extract.

- Recipes marked with a clock are quick and easy.

- *Helpful hints are marked in italics.*

- Recipes for dishes marked with an asterisk, in the entertaining section, can be found in the cookbook.

Desserts

Preceding Page: Dessert from Holiday Brunch
For Menu: See Page 234

The Cummer Museum of Art and Gardens is one of our cities finest museums. It is located in Riverside on the site of the original Cummer home. Among its treasures are world class fine art collection, an award-winning education center name Art Connection, and magnificent formal gardens.

Riverside Avenue threads its way through hospitals and homes, clinics and parks. It provides a vital link between downtown and the Riverside/ Avondale neighborhoods.

The historic homes and shady Live Oaks still line the avenue as they did in 1910.

Photograph is from collections at The Jacksonville Historical Society Archives.

BELGIAN MOCHA CAKE

1/2 cup sugar
3 tablespoons water
2 squares unsweetened
  chocolate
3/4 cup butter, softened
2 cups sugar
1 teaspoon vanilla

4 eggs, separated
2 1/4 cups flour
1/2 teaspoon baking soda
1/2 teaspoon salt
1 cup milk
1 teaspoon instant coffee
1 teaspoon cream of tartar

Preheat oven to 350°. Melt sugar, water and chocolate in double boiler or microwave oven. Cream butter and sugar. Add vanilla and egg yolks. Beat well. Stir in chocolate mixture. Combine flour, soda and salt, set aside. Stir instant coffee into milk. Add flour mixture to chocolate mixture alternating with milk mixture. In a separate bowl beat egg whites until frothy. Add cream of tartar and beat until stiff peaks form. Fold into batter. Grease three nine inch round cake pans. Line with greased wax paper and dust with flour. Pour in batter and bake at 350° for 25-30 minutes or until done. Ice with mocha frosting.

Frosting
3/4 cup butter, softened
6 cups powdered sugar
1 tablespoon cocoa

1/4 cup water
1 1/2 teaspoon cold coffee
1 1/2 teaspoon vanilla

Cream butter, sugar and cocoa until smooth. Mix water and cold coffee and add with remaining ingredients to cocoa mixture. Beat until fluffy. Frost three layer cake.

Serves: 12 to 16.

A basic cake that every dutiful wife knew by heart, way back when was called 1-2-3-4 cake. It had one pound of butter, two cups of sugar, three cups of flour, and four eggs.

CHOCOLATE TRUFFLE CAKE

Cake

8 ounces bittersweet
chocolate
1 cup butter at room
temperature

1 1/2 cup sugar
5 eggs

Preheat oven to 350°. Melt chocolate and stir until smooth.
Remove from heat and cool one to two minutes. Add butter,
bit by bit. Beat with wire whisk until smooth. Add sugar,
beating one minute with whisk. Beat eggs until foamy in a
separate bowl. Add eggs to sugar mixture and beat until well
mixed. Butter an eight inch round cake pan and line with
parchment. Pour in batter and set in slightly larger pan. Pour
hot water in the larger pan about one inch deep. Bake at 350°
for one and one-half hours. Cool one hour. Cake will fall.
Refrigerate until set, at least two hours. Invert onto cake plate
and spread with Ganache.

Ganache

12 ounces semi-sweet
chocolate

1 cup heavy cream

Boil chocolate and cream together, stirring to blend. Be
careful not to burn. Refrigerate until spreadable. Frost top
and sides of cake. Decorate top with white chocolate curls.

Serves: 8 to 10.

Skyline Jacksonville, 1927
Photograph is from collections at The Jacksonville Historical Society Archives.

$\mathscr{S}$OUR CREAM CHOCOLATE CAKE

2 cups flour
2 cups sugar
1 cup water
3/4 cup sour cream
1/4 cup shortening
1 1/4 teaspoons baking soda
1 teaspoon salt

1 teaspoon vanilla
1/2 teaspoon baking
 powder
2 eggs
4 ounces unsweetened
 chocolate, melted and
 cooled

Heat oven to 350°. Grease and flour rectangular pan, 13- by 9- by 2-inches, or two nine inch or three eight inch round cake pans. Measure all ingredients into a large mixing bowl. Mix one-half minute on low speed, scraping bowl constantly. Beat three minutes on high speed, scraping bowl occasionally. Pour into pan(s). Bake rectangular pan 40-45 minutes, layer pans 30-35 minutes or until top springs back when touched lightly with finger. Cool. Frost with Sour Cream Chocolate Frosting.

Frosting
1/3 cup butter or margarine,
 softened
3 ounces unsweetened chocolate, melted and cooled

3 cups powdered sugar
1/2 cup sour cream
2 teaspoons vanilla

Mix butter and chocolate thoroughly. Blend in sugar. Stir in sour cream and vanilla. Beat until frosting is smooth and of spreading consistency. Frost cake.

Serves: 12 to 16.

APPLE CAKE WITH PENUCHE FROSTING

2 medium eggs, slightly
  beaten
2 cups sugar
2 teaspoons vanilla extract
1/4 cup applesauce
1 cup butter
1 1/2 teaspoons baking
  soda
1/2 teaspoon salt
3 cups flour

1 1/2 teaspoons cinnamon
1/2 teaspoon nutmeg
3 cups Granny Smith apples,
  peeled, seeded and chopped

Topping
3 tablespoons butter
1/2 cup flour
1 teaspoon cinnamon
1/4 cup brown sugar

Preheat oven to 375°. Mix thoroughly in a large bowl eggs and sugar. Add vanilla, applesauce, and butter. Mix well. In a separate bowl sift together salt, baking soda, flour, cinnamon and nutmeg. Add to egg mixture and combine well. Stir in apples. Mixture will be stiff and heavy. Pour in greased and floured 12-cup tube pan. Combine topping ingredients and crumble on top of batter in tube pan. Bake for one hour. Cool and serve with Penuche Frosting.

Penuche Frosting
1/2 cup butter
1 cup firmly packed brown
  sugar

1/4 cup whole milk, heated
2 1/2 cups powdered sugar

Melt butter in sauce pan. Add brown sugar. Bring to boil. Cook seven minutes (or until slightly thickened), stirring constantly. Cool 15 minutes. Add hot milk and beat until smooth. Beat in powdered sugar until mixture is spreading consistency. Use frosting immediately.

Serves: 12 to 16.

$\mathcal{M}$EREMOM'S FAVORITE FRUITCAKE

1 pound pecans, cut into large
  pieces or halves
1 pound dates, chopped
1/2 pound candied cherries,
  cut in half (use red and
  green)
1/2 pound candied pineapple,
  cut up (use red and green)

1/2 pound candied
  pineapple, cut up, yellow
  slices
1 cup flour
1 cup sugar
1 teaspoon baking powder
4 eggs, beaten
1 teaspoon vanilla

Dredge the above ingredients in some of the flour from the one cup listed while cutting so the ingredients won't stick together. Sift the remaining flour, sugar and baking powder together. Stir in fruit. Add eggs and vanilla. Toss together until blended and coated. Grease and flour cake pan. Pour batter in pan(s). Decorate the top of the cakes with additional pineapple cherries and nuts. Use sliced pineapple slices and cut them in half so they are thinner. Put two slices on top of each loaf pan and place a whole candied cherry in the middle of each pineapple. If using one large tube pan, bake two hours at 300° starting in a cold oven with a pan of water on the lower shelf. If using two loaf pans, cook for one and one-half hours.

Sauce
1 cup orange juice   1 cup bourbon whiskey
1 cup sugar

Boil juice with sugar. Add whiskey. Pierce cake(s) with ice pick. Pour over cakes and let soak in.

These make great nostalgic Christmas gifts.

Serves: various numbers.

$\mathcal{B}$UNNY'S CARROT CAKE

2 cups flour	2 cups sugar
2 teaspoons baking soda	2 teaspoons vanilla
1/2 teaspoon salt	1 8 ounce can crushed pine-
2 teaspoons cinnamon	apple, drained
3 eggs	2 cups grated carrots
3/4 cup melted butter	1 heaping cup coconut
3/4 cup buttermilk	1 heaping cup walnuts

Preheat oven to 350°. Grease a tube pan. Sift flour, baking soda, salt and cinnamon together. Set aside. Beat eggs in large bowl. Add butter, buttermilk, sugar and vanilla. Mix well. Add flour mixture, pineapple, carrots, coconut and walnuts. Stir well. Pour into pan and bake for one hour or until toothpick comes out clean. Prepare buttermilk glaze.

Buttermilk Glaze

1 cup sugar	1 stick butter
1/2 teaspoon baking soda	1 tablespoon light corn syrup
1/2 cup buttermilk	1 teaspoon vanilla

Combine sugar, soda, buttermilk, butter and corn syrup. Bring to boil and cook five minutes, stirring occasionally. Remove from heat and stir in vanilla. Remove cake from oven and slowly pour glaze over hot cake. Cool 15 minutes. Remove from pan. Cool completely and frost.

Cream Cheese Frosting

1 stick butter, room temperature	1 teaspoon vanilla
12 ounces cream cheese, room temperature	2 cups powdered sugar

Cream butter and cream cheese. Add vanilla and powdered sugar. Mix until smooth.

Serves 12 to 16.

Cakes

NANA'S COCONUT CAKE

2 cups sugar
4 eggs
1 cup vegetable oil
1 cup milk
2 1/2 cups flour
1/2 teaspoon salt

2 1/2 teaspoons baking
  powder
1 teaspoon vanilla
seven minute icing (recipe
  follows)
2 packages fresh frozen
  coconut

Preheat oven 350°. Grease and flour three nine inch round cake pans. Beat the sugar and eggs together. Add oil, milk, flour, salt, baking powder and vanilla. Beat for one minute. Pour batter into pans. Bake 30 minutes. Prepare icing.

Seven Minute Icing
2 egg whites
1/4 cup water
1 1/2 cups sugar

1/4 teaspoon cream of
  tartar
1/8 teaspoon salt
2 teaspoons vanilla

Mix all ingredients except vanilla in the top of a double boiler (boiling water underneath). Beat steadily over low heat with hand beater until frosting stands in peaks, about five to seven minutes. Remove from heat, add vanilla, and continue to beat until thick enough to spread. Spread over bottom layer of cake, sprinkle with one third coconut; repeat for next two layers and spread completely over entire cake. Sprinkle with remaining coconut.

Serves: 12 to 16.

*O*MA'S KÜCHEN

2 cups dark brown sugar
1/2 pound butter, softened
3 cups flour
1/2 teaspoon salt
2 heaping teaspoons
cinnamon
3 teaspoons baking soda
2 eggs, beaten

1 teaspoon almond extract
3/4 cup milk
7-8 cups fresh fruit, sliced
(options: plums, peaches,
guava or apple)
cinnamon sugar (1 teaspoon
cinnamon, 2 teaspoons
sugar)

Preheat oven to 375°. Cream butter and sugar together. Add flour, salt and cinnamon. Blend well to pastry consistency. Remove one and one-half cups batter to a separate bowl and set aside. To the first bowl, add baking soda and mix well. Then add eggs, almond extract and milk. Spread in the bottom of a greased 10- by 13-inch pan. Place sliced fruit on top of batter, overlapping the sections slightly. Sprinkle with cinnamon sugar. To reserved batter, add two teaspoons butter and one-half cup brown sugar. Blend until crumbly. Sprinkle over batter and fruit. Bake about 40 minutes or until toothpick comes out clean.

Serve hot out of the pan with vanilla ice cream and caramel sauce or let cool in pan and then slice. A tasty lunch box dessert for kids or adults.

Serves: 16-20.

One summer, my grandmother, Charlotte Amanda Leicht Vaughen, visited America as a nanny for a traveling German family. On her day off, she missed the last train back to her post and was very forlorn. This got the attention of the train keeper who fell instantly in love with the little lost girl who spoke no English. He eventually traveled to Europe where he persuaded her to marry him.

My grandparents shared very robust and rewarding lives. In addition to teaching at Stetson College, they were also missionaries, Fulbright Scholars and diplomats to the Middle East.

Amid all of this, Charlotte maintained her love for German küchen. She would bake this cake for foreign dignitaries as well as for family gatherings. We all share fond memories of her kitchen and her küchen, including the one baked for my wedding. It is a recipe that can be modified to suit any occasion or taste as my grandmother's life has proven.

PRUNE CAKE WITH WHISKEY SAUCE

2 cups sugar
3/4 cup vegetable oil
3 eggs
1 1/2 teaspoons nutmeg
1 1/2 teaspoons cinnamon
1 teaspoon baking soda

1/8 teaspoon salt
1 teaspoon vanilla
1 cup buttermilk
2 cups flour
1 cup chopped prunes
1 cup chopped nuts

Preheat oven to 350°. Cream oil and sugar. Add eggs, beating after each one. Sprinkle in nutmeg, cinnamon and baking soda. Pour in vanilla. Mix in one-third of flour followed by one-third of buttermilk, alternating each one until all is included. Bake in greased and floured tube pan until done.

Whiskey Sauce
1 egg
1 cup sugar
1 tablespoon butter

1/2 cup boiling water
1/3 cup bourbon whiskey

Mix egg, sugar and butter together in the top of a double boiler. Add one-half cup boiling water. Cook on medium heat in double boiler for a few minutes. Add bourbon. Serve hot or cold. Spoon over slices of cake. It will be runny. Top with whipped cream and drizzle more sauce over cream.

Beautiful for holiday or special occasion. Serve at buffet with hot coffee.

Serves: 12 to 16.

RASPBERRY CREAM CHEESE COFFEE CAKE

2 1/2 cups flour
3/4 cup sugar
3/4 cup butter, softened
1/2 teaspoon baking powder
1/2 teaspoon baking soda
1/4 teaspoon salt
3/4 cup sour cream
1 egg

1 teaspoon almond extract
1 eight ounce package cream
  cheese, softened
1/4 cup sugar
1 egg
1/2 cup raspberry jam
1/2 cup sliced almonds

Preheat oven to 350°. In a large bowl combine flour and sugar. Cut in the butter using a pastry blender until mixture resembles coarse crumbs. Remove one cup of crumbs for topping. Add baking powder, soda, salt, sour cream, egg and almond extract to remaining crumb mixture. Blend well. Spread batter over bottom of greased and floured nine-inch springform pan. Batter should be one-quarter inch thick on all sides. In small bowl, combine cream cheese, one-quarter cup sugar and egg. Blend well. Pour over batter in the pan. Carefully spoon jam evenly over cream cheese filling. In a small bowl combine one cup of reserved flour crumbs and almonds. Sprinkle over top. Bake for 55-60 minutes or until cream cheese filling is set and crust is a deep golden brown. Cool 15 minutes. Remove sides of pan. Serve warm or cool. Cover and refrigerate leftovers.

Serves: 12 to 16.

Yacht Club 1877 at the foot of Market Street
Photograph is from collections at The Jacksonville Historical Society Archives.

LEMON, CHOCOLATE, CRANBERRY CHEESECAKE

3 tablespoons unsalted butter
1 cup graham cracker crumbs
1 cup plus one tablespoon sugar
2/3 cup semi-sweet chocolate chips
2 pounds cream cheese, at room temperature
2 tablespoons cornstarch

3 eggs, room temperature
1 teaspoon vanilla
1 cup sour cream
5 teaspoons lemon juice
2 teaspoons grated lemon zest
16 ounces whole berry cranberry sauce, about 1 1/2 cups

Heat oven to 250°. Butter a nine-inch springform pan. Melt butter and combine with graham cracker crumbs and sugar. Press into bottom of pan. Chill. Put chocolate chips in oven proof bowl and melt in oven. Let cool. Increase oven temperature to 325°. Beat cream cheese, one cup of sugar and cornstarch at medium speed until smooth. Add eggs one at a time, beating well after each addition. Beat in vanilla and sour cream. Remove two cups of batter and beat melted chocolate into it. Pour into prepared pan. Smooth top and chill. Stir four teaspoons lemon juice and one and one-half teaspoons lemon zest into remaining batter. Spoon lemon batter over chocolate batter carefully. Smooth top. Bake until toothpick stuck into center comes out just slightly moist one hour and 15 minutes to one hour and 25 minutes. Cool completely. Cover and chill. Drain cranberry sauce. Combine cranberries, remaining one teaspoon lemon juice and 1/2 teaspoon zest. Spread on top of cheesecake and refrigerate.

Yield: one nine-inch cake

$\mathcal{R}$UM RAISIN CHEESECAKE

1/2 cup golden raisins
1/2 cup dark raisins
1 1/2 tablespoons dark rum
1/4 pound lightly salted
  butter
2 cups finely ground vanilla
  wafer crumbs
1/4 cup sugar
2 pounds cream cheese,
  softened

1 1/2 cups sugar
1 teaspoon vanilla extract
1/2 teaspoon rum extract
pinch of salt
4 large eggs, room
  temperature
1 egg yolk

Preheat oven to 350°. Soak raisins in rum. Melt butter and combine with crumbs and sugar. Press crumb mixture into 10 inch springform pan, all the way up the sides and bottom. Whip cream cheese at the highest mixer speed for five minutes. Fold in sugar then beat for two more minutes. Add vanilla and rum extracts and salt, blending thoroughly. Add the eggs and egg yolk, one at a time. Keep mixer on the lowest speed. Fold in raisins and rum. Pour batter into crust and bake in preheated oven. Bake for 50 minutes. Remove from oven and let stand on counter for 10 minutes and prepare glaze.

Sour Cream Glaze
2 cups sour cream
1/4 sugar

1 teaspoon dark rum
1 teaspoon ground cloves
  (optional)

Combine sour cream, sugar and rum with rubber spatula. Spread evenly and smoothly over top of baked filling. Return to 350° oven for five minutes. Remove from oven and immediately place in refrigerator to cool and prevent cracks form forming.

Prepare at least 48 hours before serving. Store in refrigerator.

Serves: 10.

KELSEY'S ROULAGE

5 eggs, separated
1 cup powdered sugar

3 tablespoons cocoa
whipped cream

Beat yolks until pale. Add sugar and cocoa and beat again. Fold in stiffly beaten egg whites. Put in greased and floured 10 1/2 by 15 1/2 inch jelly roll pan. Bake at 350° for 15 minutes. Turn on damp cloth and roll while hot. Cool in towel. Unroll from towel. Spread with whipped cream and roll again. Slice and serve.

Serves: six.

KATHERINE'S POUND CAKE

3 cups sugar
4 1/2 sticks butter, softened
8 eggs
3 cups flour

1 teaspoon mace
1 tablespoon vanilla
1 tablespoon lemon extract

Heat oven to 300°. Cream together butter and sugar. Add eggs. Blend in flour and mace. Beat in vanilla and lemon extracts. Pour into greased and floured tube pan. Bake for one hour and 20 minutes. Let cool in pan 10 minutes and turn onto wire rack.

Serves: 12 to 16.

LAYERED SHORTBREADS

1 cup sugar
1 cup butter, softened
1 large egg
2 cups flour
1 cup finely chopped pecans
3/4 cup raspberry
  preserves

1/2 to one cup semisweet
  chocolate chips
1 teaspoon ground
  cinnamon

Preheat oven to 325°. Grease and flour an eight inch square pan. Cream sugar, butter and eggs in large bowl until light and fluffy. Stir in flour, one cup at a time until well blended. Stir in chopped pecans. Shape dough into balls and divide into two pieces. Wrap half of dough in plastic wrap while preparing remainder of recipe. Press remaining half of dough in bottom of prepared pan. Spread dough with preserves to within one-half inch of edge. Sprinkle with chocolate chips and cinnamon. Roll or pat remaining dough between sheets of wax paper to fit the size of the pan. Remove top sheet of waxed paper and invert dough over filling. Press dough lightly onto filling. Remove remaining waxed paper. Press edges to seal. Bake until golden brown, about one hour. Score top crust immediately into 16 bars then cool completely. Cut through remaining layers.

You can easily substitute your favorite preserves in this recipe.

Yield: 16 bars.

*F*AT MAN CAKES

4 eggs
1 cup butter, melted
1 teaspoon vanilla
1 box of brown sugar
1/2 cup sugar

2 cups self rising flour
1 cup pecans, chopped
3 tablespoons powdered
   sugar

Heat oven to 350°. Mix all ingredients together, one at a time, liquids first. Pour into ungreased 13-by 9-inch pan. Bake 30 minutes. Let cool in pan then cut and sprinkle with powdered sugar.

Yield: 18-24 bars.

*A*SHLEY'S CHOCOLATE CUP COOKIES

1 1/2 cups flour
1 teaspoon baking powder
1/2 teaspoon cinnamon
1 egg, beaten
1 cup ground pecans
1/2 cup butter, softened

1/2 cup sugar
1 teaspoon sherry
1 cup semi-sweet chocolate
   chips, melted
almond slivers

Heat oven to 350°. Mix together flour, baking powder, cinnamon and set aside. Cream butter and sugar in another bowl. Add egg. Fold in dry ingredients. Stir in sherry, pecans and half of the melted chocolate. Blend until dough is smooth. Roll dough out on floured surface to one-eighth inch thickness. Cut into circles with a one and one-half inch cookie cutter. Press the circles into greased, miniature cupcake pans forming a very shallow shell. Bake in preheated oven for 20 to 22 minutes. Cool on wire rack. Fill the centers with remaining melted chocolate. Insert an almond sliver in each dab of chocolate. Chill for five minutes to set chocolate.

Be careful not to overcook these delicious cookies.

Yield: three and one-half dozen cookies.

CHOCOLATE CHOCOLATE CHIP COOKIES

1 1/2 cups flour
1/2 cup unsweetened cocoa
1 teaspoon baking soda
1/2 teaspoon salt
8 ounces semi-sweet
 chocolate
4 ounces unsweetened
 chocolate

1 1/2 cups tightly packed
 light brown sugar
3/4 cup butter, softened
3 eggs
1 teaspoon vanilla
2 cups chocolate chips or
 white chocolate chunks

Heat oven to 325°. Sift together flour, cocoa, baking soda and salt. Melt together semi-sweet and unsweetened chocolate, careful not to burn. Cream together brown sugar and butter in separate bowl. Add eggs and vanilla, mixing well. Add melted chocolate, mixing well. Add dry ingredients all at one time. Mix well. Fold in two cups chocolate chips or white chocolate chunks. Drop cookies by tablespoons onto greased cookie sheets. Bake for 18-22 minutes. Cool on rack.

Yield: four to five dozen.

"The highlight of my Christmas season was cookie decorating night! Each year, my mother would include the family in the festivities of hanging the wreath, decorating the tree and, my personal favorite, decorating cookies. The year I was in the third grade, I was beside myself with excitement although my mother insisted that I take a bath before I could join in. I rushed to the bathroom, ran some water, and splashed it around without getting in. In a hurry, I ran downstairs in my robe and slippers, afraid that I might miss out on some of the fun. I might have gotten away with it, too, had not my mother spotted my dirty feet as I leapt into bed after the festivities were over!"

DOUBLE CHOCOLATE BOURBON COOKIES

2 cups flour
6 tablespoons unsweetened
  cocoa powder
1/4 teaspoon ground
  cinnamon
1/4 teaspoon salt
1 cup butter, softened
1 cup firmly packed light
  brown sugar

1/2 cup bourbon
1 cup miniature semi-sweet
  chocolate pieces
2 egg whites
2 tablespoons water
2 cups finely chopped
  pecans
1 cup coconut

Heat oven to 350°. Combine flour, cocoa powder, cinnamon and salt. Set aside. Beat butter and brown sugar together until creamy and smooth. Beat in bourbon until well blended. Add dry ingredients gradually to butter mixture, beating well after each addition. Stir in chocolate pieces. Cover dough with plastic wrap and refrigerate for at least two hours. Dough will not become completely firm, it will be sticky but workable. Grease two large cookie sheets. Beat together egg whites and water and set aside. Using level measuring tablespoon of dough, shape into balls about one inch in diameter. Roll each ball first in egg white mixture, then in chopped nuts. Arrange one-half inch apart on prepared cookie sheets. Return dough to refrigerator or freezer if necessary to firm up. Bake in preheated oven for 15 to 20 minutes or until cookies are still soft but have a light crackled crust. Cool cookies on cookie sheet for two to five minutes. Carefully remove cookies to wire rack to cool completely.

Yield: five dozen cookies.

ITALIAN WEDDING COOKIES

1/2 pound butter (1 cup)
  softened
2 cups sugar
3 eggs
1 pound ricotta cheese
4 cups flour
1 teaspoon baking soda

1 teaspoon salt
1 teaspoon vanilla
Icing
2 cups powdered sugar
1 teaspoon vanilla, may substitute almond or other extract
1/8 to 1/4 cup water

Heat oven to 350°. Cream butter and sugar. Add eggs then ricotta cheese. Mix in flour, baking soda, salt and vanilla. Drop on greased cookie sheet with a teaspoon. Bake for 12 to 15 minutes. Let cool on cookie rack. Mix together icing ingredients adding enough water to bring to spreading consistency. Glaze cooled cookies.

Glaze may be colored for a special holiday.

Yield: 100.

NUTMEG ICE BOX COOKIES

1/2 cup butter, softened
1/2 cup sugar
6 tablespoons whipping
  cream
3 tablespoons orange juice

grated rind of one orange (one
  tablespoon dried)
3 cups flour
2 teaspoons nutmeg
1/2 teaspoon salt

Cream butter with sugar in a bowl. Combine the cream, orange juice and rind and blend well. Sift the flour with nutmeg and salt, then add to the butter mixture alternately with the orange juice mixture. Add more flour, if needed, to form stiff dough. Shape into a roll and wrap in waxed paper. Chill overnight. Preheat oven to 375°. Slice one-eighth inch thick and cut a small hole with a piping tube or thimble in one side of each cookie. Place on greased baking sheet. Bake for 10 to 15 minutes or until lightly browned.

Yield: three dozen.

*M*ADELINE MAUDE'S MOLASSES COOKIES

2 3/4 cups sifted flour   1/2 cup butter
1 teaspoon baking soda   3/4 cup sugar
1/2 teaspoon salt   2 eggs
1 1/4 teaspoons cinnamon   2/3 cup light molasses
1/2 teaspoon ginger   1/2 cup milk

Heat oven to 350°. Lightly grease and flour several cookie sheets. Beat butter and sugar at medium speed. Add eggs until light and fluffy. Stir in molasses. Beat in flour mixture alternating with milk. Cover and refrigerate at least one hour. Drop by teaspoons, two inches apart on cookie sheet. Bake for 10 minutes until surface springs back when touched lightly. Remove to wire rack. Cool completely.

Ginger Cream
1/2 cup butter, softened   2 tablespoons of milk
3 cups confectioners sugar   1/4 cup light molasses
1 1/4 teaspoons ginger

Beat all ingredients until smooth. Spread between cooled cookies to make sandwiches.

My mother only made these once, but I remembered them into adulthood.

Yield: two dozen.

The Powell sisters, A Tom Thumb Wedding

OTHER MAGEE'S

MANDARIN ORANGE COOKIES

2/3 cup butter, softened
3/4 cup sugar
1 egg
1/2 cup orange juice
2 tablespoons grated orange
  peel

2 cups flour
1/2 teaspoon baking
  powder
1/2 teaspoon soda
1/4 teaspoon salt
orange icing (recipe follows)

Heat oven to 400°. Mix butter, egg and sugar until creamed. Stir in juice and zest. Blend dry ingredients together and add to batter. Drop rounded teaspoons of dough onto ungreased cookie sheets. Leave about two inches between cookies. Bake eight to ten minutes until edges are lightly browned. Do not over bake. Frost with icing while warm.

Orange Icing
3 tablespoons butter, softened
1 1/2 cups powdered sugar
1 1/2 tablespoons orange
  juice

2 teaspoons grated orange
  peel

Blend butter and sugar until smooth. Add remaining ingredients until creamy.

These cookies taste great for a relaxed patio party on a clear day.

Yield: three and one-half to four dozen cookies.

PATTI'S WORLD'S BEST COOKIES

1 cup butter, softened	1/2 teaspoon salt
1 cup sugar	1 teaspoon baking soda
1 cup brown sugar	1 teaspoon vanilla
1 egg	1 cup crushed corn flakes
1 cup oil	1/2 cup shredded coconut
1 cup oatmeal	1/2 cup finely chopped
3 1/2 cups flour	pecans

Heat oven to 350°. Mix butter, egg and sugar until creamed. Add egg, oil, corn flakes, oatmeal, pecans and coconut. Stir and mix well. Blend in vanilla, flour, salt and baking soda. Roll into small balls and place on ungreased cookie sheets. Flatten with fork dipped in warm water. Bake for 10 to 12 minutes until lightly browned.

All the men I know who have tasted these come back for more.

Yield: 10-12 dozen cookies.

PECAN MACAROONS

1 egg white	1 teaspoon vanilla
3/4 cup brown sugar	2 cups pecans

Beat egg white until stiff. Add sugar and vanilla. Mix well. Drop in pecans. Dip out with fork or drop by teaspoon on greased cookie sheet. Bake 10 minutes at 325° or 20 minutes at 300°.

Yield: about two dozen.

"My mother learned to hide the refrigerated oatmeal dough because as a child I could sniff it out and would consume it before she could even get it in the oven!"

CINNAMON HONEY SQUARES

2 cups flour
1 1/2 teaspoons cinnamon
1 teaspoon baking soda
1/2 teaspoon salt
1 egg, beaten

3/4 cup oil
1/2 cup honey
1 cup sugar
1 cup chopped pecans

Sift together flour, cinnamon, baking soda and salt. Mix in egg, oil, honey, sugar and pecans. Spread on greased 10 by 15-inch jelly roll pan. Bake 20 minutes. Top while still warm with glaze. Cut into squares.

Glaze
1 cup powdered sugar
1 tablespoon water

2 tablespoons mayonnaise
1 teaspoon vanilla

Mix together and spread on squares.

Yield: six dozen squares.

AUNT ELOISE'S PECAN SQUARES

Crust
2/3 cup powdered sugar

2 cups flour
1 cup butter, softened

Preheat oven to 350°. Grease and flour a 9- by 13-inch pan. Sift sugar and flour together. Cut in butter until fine crumbs form. Pat crust into prepared pan. Bake for 20 minutes.

Topping
2/3 cup melted butter
1/2 cup honey
3 tablespoons heavy cream

1/2 cup brown sugar
3 1/2 cups chopped pecans
1 cup semi-sweet chocolate
  chips (optional)

Mix together butter, honey, cream, brown sugar and chocolate chips. Stir in pecans, coating them thoroughly. Spread topping carefully over crust. Return to oven and bake for 25 minutes. Cool completely before cutting into squares.

Yield: 36 squares.

Aunt Eloise wraps her pecan squares individually in wax paper and tucks them in the pockets of her husband's jacket when he goes quail hunting.

 ARAMEL, OAT AND CHOCOLATE BARS

1 1/2 cup flour
1 1/2 cups firmly packed
   brown sugar
1 1/2 cups old fashion oats
1/2 teaspoon baking soda
1/4 teaspoon salt
3/4 cup unsalted butter,
   chilled and cut into pieces

12 ounces of semi-sweet
   chocolate chips
1 cup chopped walnuts or
   pecans
1/2 cup whipping cream
14 ounces caramel pieces,
   unwrapped

Combine flour, brown sugar, oats, baking soda and salt in food processor. Add butter and cut in using on and off turns until crumbs form. Press all but two cups of the crumb mixture into bottom of a 9- by 13- inch pan. Sprinkle with chocolate chips and nuts. Set crust aside. Bring cream to simmer in heavy, medium saucepan over medium heat. Add caramels and stir until melted and smooth. Pour caramel mixture over crust. Sprinkle reserved two cups of crumb mixture over caramel mixture. Bake until edges are lightly brown. Cut around sides to loosen. Cool completely. Cut into bars. Refrigerate until well chilled, at least three hours. Serve cold.

Yield: 20.

ℬUTTER PECAN ICE CREAM

1 cup chopped pecans
1 tablespoon butter
5 eggs
1/4 cup sugar
1 14-ounce can sweetened
   condensed milk
1 teaspoon vanilla

2 teaspoons butter flavoring
1/4 teaspoon maple flavoring
dash of salt
1 small package instant vanilla
   pudding
3 quarts whole milk

Toast pecans in butter in oven at 300° for 10 minutes, no longer. Beat eggs and sugar together. Add remaining ingredients. Pour in enough half and half to make one gallon. Put in one gallon ice cream freezer bucket and freeze until firm.

Yield: one gallon.

ℱUDGY CHOCOLATE ICE CREAM

10 ounces unsweetened
   chocolate, melted
28 ounces sweetened con-
   densed milk
4 egg yolks

4 teaspoons vanilla
4 cups half and half
4 cups whipping cream
2 cups chopped macadamia
   nuts

Beat chocolate, condensed milk, egg yolks and vanilla in large mixing bowl. Stir in half and half, whipping cream and nuts. Pour into ice cream freezer container and freeze according to manufacturer's direction. Store leftovers in freezer.

Yield: three quarts.

*L*EMON VELVET ICE CREAM

1 quart plus 1 1/3 cups whipping cream	4 cups sugar
1 quart plus 1 1/3 cups milk	2 teaspoons lemon extract
juice of 8 lemons	1 tablespoon grated lemon rind

Mix thoroughly and freeze in electric freezer according to manufacturer's directions.

Yield: one gallon.

*P*EPPERMINT STICK ICE CREAM

9 eggs	1 1/2 tablespoons vanilla
4 cups sugar	1 cup crushed peppermint candy
6 cups cream	
10 cups milk	

Beat eggs and milk together in large saucepan. Add sugar. Cook over low heat, stirring constantly until thickened, about 15 minutes. Mixture will coat the spoon. Cool. Add cream and vanilla. Refrigerate overnight. Crush one cup of peppermint stick candy between two dish towels. Add candy and a few drops of red food coloring to cream mixture. Freeze in electric freezer according to manufacturer's directions.

Yield: one and one-half gallons.

My mom had gotten remarried and I wasn't sure about my new dad. For as long as I could remember, my family had been limited to my mom, my sister and me. I didn't want things to change. One Saturday afternoon, Mom decided to make ice cream. Homemade ice cream was one of the things we all loved. Mom sent me outside with a hammer and peppermints wrapped in a towel so that we would have crushed candies for the recipe. Well, my new dad was also outside setting up the freezer with rock salt and testing the blades. We didn't say a whole lot to each other as we worked on our individual jobs, but we had a common goal. I decided that if we could share ice cream, that maybe we could share Mom, too.

CHOCOLATE PECAN PIE

3/4 cup sugar
1/2 teaspoon salt
1 cup light corn syrup
3 1-ounce squares unsweet-
    ened chocolate, melted
    and cooled

3 tablespoons butter or
    regular margarine, melted
3 eggs
1 teaspoon vanilla
1 cup chopped pecans
1 9-inch unbaked pie shell

Preheat oven 375°. Combine sugar, salt, corn syrup, cooled chocolate, butter, eggs and vanilla in bowl. Beat with mixer at medium speed till well blended. Stir in pecans. Turn mixture into pie shell. Bake 35 minutes or until set. Pie is high and fluffy when it comes out of the oven, but sinks in the center while cooling on rack.

Yield: one nine-inch pie.

CUSTARD PECAN PIE

1/2 cup butter
2 cups sugar
2 teaspoons vanilla
3 eggs
3 tablespoons flour

1/4 teaspoon salt
1 cup buttermilk
1/2 cup chopped pecans
1 9-inch unbaked pie shell

Preheat oven to 300°. Cream butter and sugar, adding one-half cup sugar at a time. Blend vanilla. Add eggs, one at a time. Combine flour and salt, add small amount at a time. Add buttermilk. Sprinkle the pecans in bottom of pie crust. Pour custard mix over pecans and bake one hour 30 minutes. Serve at room temperature.

Yield: one nine-inch pie.

KATE'S BLACK BOTTOM PIE

1 tablespoon unflavored
gelatin
4 tablespoons cold water
2 cups milk
1 1/2 cups milk
1/2 cup sugar

1 tablespoon cornstarch
1/4 teaspoon salt
4 egg yolks, beaten
2 ounces (2 squares) unsweetened chocolate, melted
1 teaspoon vanilla

Soften gelatin in cold water. Scald milk in double boiler. Mix sugar, cornstarch and salt together; stir slowly into milk and cook until thick. Add gradually to beaten egg yolks. Return to double boiler and cook three minutes longer. Stir in gelatin to dissolve. Remove one cup and add melted chocolate and vanilla to it to make chocolate layer. Pour carefully into Gingersnap Crust.

Gingersnap Crust
35 gingersnaps
1/4 pound butter, melted

1 tablespoon powdered sugar

Preheat oven at 300°. Roll gingersnaps with rolling pin to make fine crumbs. Add melted butter and sugar and mix well. Press firmly into a nine inch pie tin. Bake for five minutes.

Cream Layer
4 egg whites
1/8 teaspoon cream of tartar
1/2 cup sugar

1 tablespoon rum
1 teaspoon sherry
3/4 cup heavy cream
1 tablespoon shaved unsweetened chocolate

Let remaining custard cool. Beat egg whites until frothy; add cream of tartar; continue beating to a soft peak, and gradually add sugar. Fold meringue into cooled custard; add flavorings. Pour carefully over chocolate layer. Chill in refrigerator until set. When ready to serve, whip cream, spread on top of pie, and sprinkle with shaved chocolate.

Yield: one nine-inch pie.

$\mathcal{D}$ATE NUT PUMPKIN PIE

Crust
1 1/2 cups flour
1/2 teaspoon salt
1/2 cup shortening
4 to 5 tablespoons cold water
Date-Nut Layer
1 8-ounce package pitted
  dates, chopped
3/4 cup water
1/3 cup packed brown sugar
4 tablespoons margarine or
  butter
1/2 cup walnuts, chopped
1/2 teaspoon ground
  cinnamon

Pumpkin Filling
2 large eggs
1 16-ounce can solid pack
  pumpkin
1 cup evaporated milk
1/2 cup sugar
1/2 cup packed brown sugar
1/2 teaspoon ground cinnamon
1/2 teaspoon ground ginger
1/2 teaspoon ground nutmeg
1/4 teaspoon salt
1/8 teaspoon ground cloves

Mix flour and salt for crust in medium bowl. Cut in shortening with pastry blender or two knives used scissor-fashion,
until mixture resembles coarse crumbs. Stir in water, one
tablespoon at a time, until dough forms a ball. Wrap in plastic
wrap and refrigerate while preparing date-nut layer and
filling. Heat chopped pitted dates and water to boiling, in
two quart saucepan over medium heat. Cook, stirring frequently, until dates have softened. Stir in brown sugar and
margarine or butter until blended. Remove saucepan from
heat; stir in chopped walnuts and ground cinnamon. Cool
while preparing filling. Beat eggs lightly for filling, in medium saucepan with a wire whisk or fork. Stir in solid pack
pumpkin and remaining filling ingredients until well
blended. Preheat oven to 450°. Roll three-quarters of the
dough on lightly floured surface, with floured rolling pin,
into a round, about one inch larger than a nine inch inverted
pie plate. Ease dough into pie plate. Trim edge even with pie
plate. Reserve trimmings. Pour date-nut mixture into crust.
Top with pumpkin filling. Roll reserved trimmings and
remaining one-quarter of dough one-eighth inch thick. With
knife or cookie cutter, cut out a three inch pumpkin design
and a few leaves. Arrange on top of pumpkin filling. Cut out

small leaves with knife or small cookie cutter. Moisten pie
crust edge with water; press small leaves all around edge of
pie. Bake pie 10 minutes. Turn oven down to 350° and bake
35 minutes longer or until knife inserted in center of pie
comes out clean. Cool and serve.

Serves: 10.

LEMON MERINGUE PIE

1 homemade or store-bought graham cracker crust	2 egg yolks, beaten
1/2 cup fresh lemon juice	Meringue:
1 teaspoon grated lemon rind	4 egg whites
1 can condensed milk	1/4 teaspoon cream of tartar
	4 tablespoons sugar

Preheat oven at 325°. Combine lemon juice and rind. Gradually stir in condensed milk and add egg yolks slowly. Blend
well. Pour mixture into crust. Beat egg whites and cream of
tartar until stiff peaks form. Add sugar slowly. Spoon onto
top of pie mixture and bake until meringue is golden brown.
Refrigerate.

Yield: one nine-inch pie.

STRAWBERRY COCONUT PIE

2 1/2 cups flaked coconut (toasted)	2 1/2 cups strawberries (mashed)
1/3 cup butter	3 teaspoons lemon concentrate
1 3-ounce package soft cream cheese	1 cup (1/2 pint) whipping cream, whipped
1 14-ounce sweetened condensed milk	

Combine coconut and butter. Press firmly into a nine inch pie
plate. Beat cheese until fluffy, with mixer in large bowl.
Gradually beat in condensed milk. Stir in lemon and strawberries. Fold in whipped cream. Freeze four hours and serve.

Serves: six to eight.

MINI-APRICOT PIES

Meat
6 onces dried apricots
3/4 cup water
1/2 teaspoon nutmeg
1/2 teaspoon cinnamon,
  ground
1/2 teaspoon cloves, ground
1/2 teaspoon vanilla extract
Dough
1/2 cup butter, softened
4 ounces cream cheese,
  softened

1/2 teaspoon salt
1 1/2 cup flour
Glaze
1 cup sifted powdered sugar
1 1/2 teaspoons milk
1/2 teaspoon vanilla extract
1/4 teaspoon butter flavored
  extract or 1/2 teaspoon
  apricot brandy
1 teaspoon cinnamon

Preheat oven at 350°. Chop apricots until fine. Combine meat ingredients. In a saucepan, cook over medium heat for five minutes, stirring constantly. Set aside. Beat butter and cream cheese until smooth. Add flour and salt. Beat until dough forms a ball. Roll out dough to one-eighth inch thickness on a lightly floured surface. Cut into two and one-half inch circles using biscuit cutter. Place about one teaspoon apricot meat to one side of center. Moisten edges with water and fold dough over to form a crescent shape. Press edges to seal. Crimp edges with fork and prick top of each. Place on greased cookie sheet. Bake for 10 to 20 minutes or until browned on bottom oven rack. Remove to wire rack. Brush with glaze when cool.

Yield: two to three dozen.

ORANGE CHESS PIE

3 eggs
1/4 cup fresh squeezed orange
 juice
1 cup flaked coconut
6 tablespoons butter

1 1/2 cups sugar
1 teaspoon vanilla
1 unbaked nine-inch pie
 shell

Preheat oven at 350°. Mix all ingredients, except pie shell, together and pour into unbaked pie shell. Bake for approximately 45 minutes.

Yield: one nine-inch pie.

PUMPKIN ICE CREAM PIE

1 ready-made or home-made
 graham cracker crust pie
 shell
1 quart premium vanilla ice
 cream
1 cup pumpkin puree

1/2 cup brown sugar
1/2 teaspoon salt
1/2 teaspoon ginger
1/2 teaspoon cinnamon
1/4 teaspoon nutmeg

Thaw ice cream and blend in all ingredients except pie shell. Fill pie shell and re-freeze. Cover the ice cream pie to protect it in the freezer.

Yield: one nine-inch pie.

View of pier and Atlantic Beach Hotel at Atlantic Beach.
Photograph is from collections at The Beaches Area Historical Society Archives.

$\mathcal{R}$HUBARB, APPLE AND PINEAPPLE PIE

Crust

2 cups flour	2/3 cup shortening
1 teaspoon salt	4 to 5 tablespoons cold water
1/2 teaspoon baking powder	

Filling

1 or 2 medium-sized McIntosh apples, peeled and diced (about 1 cup)	1 cup sugar
	1/4 cup honey
	3 tablespoons flour
1 8-ounce can crushed pine- apple, drained	1 teaspoon lemon juice
	1/8 teaspoon salt
3 cups fresh or frozen unsweetened rhubarb	1 tablespoon margarine or butter

For crust, combine flour, salt and baking powder in medium bowl. Cut in shortening, with pastry blender or two knives used scissor-fashion, until mixture resembles coarse crumbs. Stir in water, one tablespoon at a time, until mixture forms ball. Divide dough in half; wrap and refrigerate until ready to use. Mix all filling ingredients except margarine or butter in large bowl. Preheat oven to 450°. Roll half of dough one inch larger all around than inverted nine inch pie plate on lightly floured surface, with floured rolling pin. Ease dough into pie plate. Spoon filling into crust; dot filling with margarine or butter. Roll remaining dough as for bottom crust. Cut into 10 three-fourths inch-wide strips. Moisten edge of bottom crust with water. Use pastry strips to weave a lattice over filling. Press each strip at both ends to seal. Turn overhang up over ends of strips; pinch to seal; flute. Place pie in oven; immediately turn oven control to 350°. Bake one to one and one-quarter hours until filling in center is bubbly and crust is golden brown. Cool and serve.

Serves: 10.

*A*MY'S FROZEN RASPBERRY SOUFFLE

12 egg yolks
2 1/4 cups sugar, divided
1 cup pureed and strained
  fresh raspberries
2/3 cup whipping cream,
  whipped
8 egg whites, room
  temperature

pinch of salt
sweetened whipped cream
  and fresh raspberries
  (garnish)
Sabayon sauce or Créme
  Fraîche

Beat yolks in large bowl until thick and lemon colored. Add one and one-quarter cups sugar and beat until dissolved. Transfer to double boiler, place over hot water and cook until custard coats metal spoon; do not allow to boil at anytime. Strain into large metal bowl set over ice and stir until cool. Add raspberries a little at a time, blending thoroughly after each addition. Fold whipped cream into mixture. Beat egg whites in a large bowl with salt until soft peak forms. Gradually beat in remaining sugar, two tablespoons at a time. Mix one-third egg whites into custard to loosen, then gently fold in remaining whites. Pour into prepared dish, smooth top with spatula and freeze overnight. When firm, cover top with plastic wrap or foil. Just before serving, garnish with whipped cream fresh berries and accompany with Créme Fraîche or Sabayon.

Créme Fraîche
2 teaspoons cultured
  buttermilk

2 cups whipping cream

Mix whipping cream and buttermilk in sauce pan and heat to 85°. Let sauce stand until thickened, keeping temperature between 60° and 85°. Stir gently and refrigerate until ready to use.

Serves: 10 to 12.

$\mathcal{W}$INKIE'S TIRAMISU

1 16-ounce container
mascarpone cheese*
1/2 teaspoon salt
2 tablespoons powered sugar
3 tablespoons coffee-flavored
liqueur
1 1/3 teaspoons vanilla
3 1-ounce squares semi-sweet
chocolate, coarsely grated
1 1/2 cups heavy or
whipping cream
2 teaspoons instant espresso-
coffee powder
2 3 to 4 1/2-ounce
packages ladyfingers

Beat mascarpone, salt, three tablespoons coffee-liqueur, one teaspoon vanilla extract and two-thirds of grated chocolate in a large bowl with wire whisk or fork. (Set aside remaining chocolate for top of dessert.) Beat one cup heavy or whipping cream, in small bowl, with mixer at medium speed, until soft peaks form. Fold whipped cream into cheese mixture with rubber spatula or wire whisk. Stir instant espresso powder, one-third teaspoon vanilla and two tablespoons water in small bowl. Separate ladyfingers into halves. Line 10-cup glass or crystal bowl with one-fourth of ladyfingers, brush with two tablespoons espresso mixture. Spoon one-third of cheese mixture to make two more layers. Top with remaining ladyfingers, gently pressing ladyfingers into cheese mixture. Brush ladyfingers with remaining espresso mixture. Sprinkle remaining grated chocolate over top of dessert, reserving one table-spoon for garnish. Beat remaining one-half cup heavy or whipping cream and two tablespoons confectioners' sugar, in small bowl, with mixer at medium speed, until soft peaks form. Spoon whipped-cream mixture into decorating bag with large star tube. Pipe large rosettes on top of dessert. Sprinkle reserved grated chocolate on rosettes. Cover dessert and refrigerate at least two hours to chill to blend flavors.

If mascarpone cheese is not available, substitute two eight ounce packages cream cheese, softened. In a large bowl, with mixer at medium speed, beat cream cheese and three tablespoons milk until smooth and fluffy.

Serves: 16.

"What is that glorious smell?" As a child, I can remember dashing in the front door of my Mema's house in wondrous anticipation of what mouth-watering delicacy she would be baking today! Would it be smiling gingerbread men, sugar cookie wreaths, spiced with nutmeg, yummy chocolaty fudge, crunchy mints the size of quarters or pralines laden with pecans? Mema had a schedule posted on her refrigerator for the days leading up to the big Holiday celebration. Alongside this list of future delights would be the recipe of the day splattered with past bits of batter from an overzealous grandchild, me! We always said that you could pick out the best recipes by looking at those that had the most evidence of loving use. Somehow those days of the Holiday season would find various members of the family stopping by Mema's house for a whiff and a taste of her latest labor of love. When I close my eyes, I can still see, smell and hug those wonderful Holiday memories."

Feeding ducks at Riverside Park. Completed in 1894.
Photograph is from collections at The Jacksonville Historical Society Archives.

GINGERBREAD ROLL WITH LEMON FILLING

4 large eggs, separated
1/2 cup sugar
1/3 cup molasses
3/4 cup flour
1/2 teaspoon baking powder
1/2 teaspoon baking soda
3/4 teaspoon ground ginger
3/4 teaspoon ground
  cinnamon
1/4 teaspoon ground
  allspice
1/4 teaspoon ground
  cloves
2 tablespoons powdered
  sugar
Lemon filling
1 tablespoon powdered
  sugar

Preheat oven at 375°. Grease bottom and sides of a 15- by 10- by 1-inch jellyroll pan with vegetable oil; line with wax paper. Set aside. Beat egg yolks at high speed with an electric mixer until thickened. Gradually add sugar, beating until thick. Stir in molasses. Combine flour, baking powder, baking soda, ginger, cinnamon, allspice and cloves. Gradually add to egg mixture, mixing until blended. Beat egg whites until stiff peaks form, then gently fold into batter. Spread evenly into pan. Bake for 10 to 12 minutes or until cake springs back when lightly touched. Cool in pan on a wire rack for five minutes. Sift two tablespoons powdered sugar in a 15- by 10- inch rectangle on a cloth towel. Loosen cake from sides of pan using a small metal spatula. Turn cake out onto sugared towel and carefully peel off wax paper. Starting at narrow end, roll up cake and towel together. Cool completely on a wire rack, seam side down. Unroll cake and remove towel. Spread with Lemon Filling and carefully re-roll. Chill two hours. Sprinkle with one tablespoon powdered sugar before serving.

Lemon Filling
3/4 cup sugar
2 tablespoons cornstarch
2/3 cup water
1/4 cup lemon juice
2 egg yolks, beaten
1 3-ounce package cream
  cheese, softened
2 tablespoons butter or
  margarine, softened

Combine sugar and cornstarch in a small saucepan. Add water, lemon juice and egg yolks gradually. Bring to a boil, stirring constantly. Boil one minute. Remove from heat. Beat cream cheese and butter at medium speed with an electric mixer until blended. Add hot mixture slowly, beating until smooth. Chill about 30 minutes or until mixture reaches spreading consistency, stirring occasionally.

Yield: 1 2/3 cups.

Cake may be prepared and stored in the refrigerator 24 hours before serving.

Serves: 8 to 10.

CHOCOLATE FLAN

1 cup water
4 egg yolks (beat in separate bowl)
2 egg whites (beat in separate bowl)
4 squares semi-sweet chocolate

2 14-ounce cans condensed milk
1 teaspoon vanilla
1 tablespoon dark rum
whipping cream

Melt chocolate in water; set to cool. Pour two cans of condensed milk in a bowl. Add eggs and beat lightly. Add chocolate, vanilla and rum. Pour into greased loaf pan. Put loaf pan in a separate deep pan of water and fill up one-quarter of pan with water. Bake at 350° for one hour. It is important to cook flan in the pan of water. After it cools, scrape around loaf pan with knife. Flip out carefully. Top may not all come out evenly. Refrigerate. Cut out small squares and top with whipping cream.

Yield: 20 small squares.

DECADENT DATE PUDDING

Batter
1 cup flour
1/2 cup sugar
2 teaspoons baking powder
1 egg
1/4 scant cup milk
1 cup chopped fresh dates or
  boxed chopped dates
1 cup coarsely chopped
  pecans or walnuts

Filling
2 cups sugar
2 cups boiling water
2 tablespoons butter,
  softened
1 teaspoon vanilla
Chantilly Cream
1/2 cup cream
1 tablespoon sugar
1/2 teaspoon vanilla or
  favorite liqueur

Preheat oven at 350°. Combine flour, sugar, baking powder, egg and milk in a medium bowl. Add dates and nuts. The batter will be very stiff. Spread in a thin, even layer across the bottom of a lightly buttered 9- by 13-inch baking pan. Combine sugar and boiling water for filling in a pour-spout bowl, stirring until sugar dissolves. Whisk in butter and vanilla. Pour over date batter. Bake 45 minutes, until golden brown. The pudding will rise to the top and the filling will sink to the bottom. In a cold bowl with cold beaters, whip cream, sugar and vanilla for the Chantilly Cream to moderately stiff peaks. Chill, covered, until ready for use. Cool the date pudding thoroughly. Cut into big squares. Top each square with a dollop of Chantilly Cream. *To keep dates from sticking, chop with a chef's knife, with a blade six to eight inches long dusted with powdered sugar, or cut dates with scissors.*

Serves: eight.

FROZEN ORANGE CUSTARDS

3 large egg yolks
1/3 cup sugar
3/4 teaspoon freshly grated
  orange zest
1 cup heavy cream, well
  chilled
1/2 teaspoon vanilla

2 tablespoons thawed
  orange juice concentrate
1 pint fresh raspberries or
  blackberries sweetened in
  1/4 cup sugar and 1
  tablespoon kirsch
  (optional)

Beat yolks for five seconds in the bowl of electric mixer. Add sugar, a little at a time, and zest. Beat the mixture until it is thick and pale. Beat the cream in a chilled bowl with the vanilla, until it forms soft peaks and fold in the yolk mixture and the orange juice concentrate. Gently, but thoroughly, divide the mixture among eight one-half cup ramekins. Cover them with plastic wrap and freeze for at least four hours. Dip the ramekins in hot water; run a thin knife around each custard and invert the custards on to dessert plates. Spoon raspberries over custard.

Serves: eight.

Couples dancing inside dance pavilion at Jacksonville Beach Pier.
Photograph is from collections at The Beaches Area Historical Society Archives.

SUMMERHOUSE FUDGE PUDDING

4 cups sugar
1 cup flour
1 cup cocoa
8 large eggs

2 cups butter, melted
4 teaspoons vanilla
2 cups chopped pecans

Preheat oven to 300°. Sift together sugar, flour and cocoa. Beat eggs in large mixing bowl. Add dry ingredients, butter and vanilla. Mix well. Stir in pecans and pour into three quart Pyrex dish. Place in water bath* and bake on oven shelf at lowest level for one hour and 20 minutes. DON'T OVER-BAKE. Remove from water bath and cool completely on wire rack. Top becomes crusty as pudding cools.

For a water bath, place your baking dish in a jelly roll pan and fill pan to about three-quarters full with tap water. Let both containers bake on oven shelf this way. It is good to place them on oven shelf and use your tea kettle to fill the pan.

A small serving of this wonderful dessert served in a pretty little bowl or a silver or crystal stem is divine. For a delicious rich treat, top with coffee ice cream and garnish with a plump strawberry!

Serves: 16-24.

Halimar Lodge is a place I have never been. It is tucked away on the shores of Lake Kashagawigamog. A vacation resort, it has changed over the years as have most things. But, it exists in my husband's memories just as it did in the late fifties. It is his place of childhood innocence, where his dreams were formed and family friendships bonded.

The dining hall was the social center for the lodgers' activities. Families played cribbage, read their mail, entered talent contests and told tall tales around its tables. It also served some of the best family-style food around. One of the favorites being its fudge pudding. "One serving per person" was the rule, but my husband always found a way to get more. Now that was good living.

I can't visit Halimar Lodge. My childhood is somewhere else. But, I can make fudge pudding. When my husband goes back for a second helping. I know where he is, reliving the laughter now muted and friendships faded, dreams realized and innocence reborn.

$\mathcal{M}$AMA'S RICE PUDDING

3 eggs
2 1/2 cups milk
1/2 cup sugar
1/4 cup brown sugar
dash cinnamon and nutmeg

1 teaspoon vanilla
salt to taste
1 cup cooked rice
1 cup seedless raisins

Preheat oven to 350°. Beat eggs; pour in all ingredients with rice into greased two-quart casserole. Bake for one hour.

Serves: six.

$\mathcal{B}$LAZING SUNDAE

1 scoop ice cream
1 tablespoon chocolate or
   butterscotch topping

1 sugar cube
1 teaspoon lemon extract
1 large marshmallow

Place the scoop of ice cream in a serving bowl and top with topping. Soak sugar cube with lemon extract. Make a small, sugar-cube size, well in marshmallow. Push the soaked cube onto the marshmallow and then push the marshmallow into the ice cream. If the ice cream is hard, first make a marshmallow-size well in the ice cream with a teaspoon. Tell everyone to stand back, light the sugar cube and impress!

For the Fourth of July, use strawberry ice cream, topped with whipped cream and blueberry syrup. Kids love this!

Serves: one.

$\mathscr{P}$UMPKIN CREME BRULEE

2 1/4 cup heavy cream
1/2 cup light cream
1 teaspoon vanilla
1 16 oz can pumpkin puree
1 cup sugar
1 teaspoon ground ginger

1/2 teaspoon cinnamon
1/2 teaspoon ground allspice
1/4 teaspoon ground cloves
1/2 teaspoon salt
6 extra large eggs
1/2 cup soft brown sugar

Preheat oven at 350°. Combine creams in saucepan. Add vanilla and bring to boil. Remove from heat immediately and let cool 15 minutes. Whisk pumpkin, white sugar, salt, spices and eggs in large bowl. Whisk cream into pumpkin mixture. Pour into quiche pan and bake in bain-marie (water bath) until just set, about 30 to 40 minutes. Remove from oven. Spread brown sugar on top of baked custard and heat under broiler until sugar is caramelized and crisp. Chill well before serving.

Serves: six to eight.

 # $\mathscr{D}$AVIS' FROZEN YOGURT POPS

1 6-ounce can frozen orange
  juice concentrate
1 12-ounce can evaporated
  skimmed milk
2 8-ounce containers strawberry low-fat yogurt (about
  2 cups)

1 tablespoon honey
15 3-ounce size paper cups
15 wooden sticks

Place juice concentrate, milk, yogurt and honey in blender. Cover and blend on medium-high speed five to 10 seconds. Divide among paper cups. Freeze 30 minutes. Insert wooden sticks in centers of cups. Freeze at least eight hours until firm. Remove paper cups before serving.

Also great with six ounces limeade and two eight-ounce containers cappuccino yogurt.

Yield: 15 pops.

HOLIDAY SORBET

1 12-ounce package fresh or
frozen cranberries
1 1/2 cups orange juice
1 cup water
2/3 cup sugar
2 tablespoons orange fla-
vored liqueur (optional)
1 3/4 cups water

1/3 cup sugar
1 1/2 teaspoons lemon juice
1 16-ounce can frozen limeade
concentrate, thawed and
undiluted
garnishes: fresh mint sprigs,
fresh cranberries

Combine cranberries, orange juice, water and sugar in a large
saucepan. Bring to a boil. Cover, reduce heat and simmer six
to eight minutes or until cranberry skins pop. Cool 10 minutes. Position knife blade in food processor bowl. Add half of
cranberry mixture; process until smooth, stopping once to
scrape down sides. Repeat procedure. Pour mixture through
a large, wire-mesh strainer, discarding pulp then stir in liqueur, if desired. Pour into a 13- by 9- by 2-inch pan. Freeze
mixture until firm. Combine one and three-quarters cups
water and one-third cup sugar in a saucepan. Cook over
medium heat, stirring constantly, until sugar dissolves. Remove from heat, and stir in lemon juice and limeade concentrate. Pour into an eight inch square pan and freeze until firm.
Position knife blade in processor bowl; add lime mixture, and
process until smooth. Set aside. Process half of frozen cranberry mixture until smooth and spread into a 9- by 5- by 3-
inch loafpan. Process remaining cranberry mixture, set aside.
Spoon lime mixture over cranberry mixture in pan, spreading
evenly. Spread remaining cranberry mixture on top. Cover
and freeze until firm. Remove from pan and cut into slices.
Serve with commercial cookies and garnish, if desired.

Serves: eight.

$\mathcal{V}$ANILLA CREAM WITH RASPBERRIES

1 envelope unflavored
   gelatin
1/2 cup cold water
2 cups whipping cream
3/4 cup sugar

2 cups sour cream
1 teaspoon vanilla extract
2 cups fresh or frozen
   raspberries, thawed
1/4 cup amaretto

Sprinkle gelatin over cold water in a small saucepan. Let stand one minute. Cook over low heat, stirring until gelatin dissolves, about two minutes. Set mixture aside. Combine whipping cream and sugar in a medium saucepan. Cook over low heat, stirring until sugar dissolves and mixture is no longer grainy. Remove from heat, and stir in gelatin mixture, sour cream and vanilla. Pour into a one and one-half quart serving bowl. Cover and refrigerate eight hours. Combine raspberries and amaretto and let stand 15 minutes. Just before serving, spoon chilled cream into dessert bowls and top with raspberries.

Serves: 8 to 10.

The Stockton Family. Riverside at Stockton.
Photograph is from collections at The Riverside/Avondale Preservation Archives.

AVLOVA

4 large egg whites
1/8 teaspoon salt
1 cup sugar
1 tablespoon cornstarch
1 teaspoon vanilla

1 teaspoon white vinegar
2 cups heavy cream
4 kiwi fruit, peeled and sliced
Raspberry Sauce
   (recipe follows)

Preheat oven 250°. Line a cookie sheet with piece of foil.
Mark an eight inch circle and dust with cornstarch. In large
bowl at high speed, beat egg whites and salt untill frothy.
Mix one tablespoon sugar and one tablespoon cornstarch.
Set aside. Gradually add remaining sugar to egg whites
untill blended; add sugar-cornstarch and beat till stiff. Add
vanilla and vinegar. Spread on cookie sheet within marked
circle, spooning higher on sides to form hollow. Bake one
and one-half hours. Turn off oven, open door, and let set in
oven five minutes. Cool completely on wire rack. Peel off foil
and slide onto serving platter. Just before serving, whip
cream untill stiff. Flavor to taste. Line center of meringue
shell with the kiwi fruit and top with whipped cream. Serve
with raspberry sauce. Keep chilled.

Raspberry Sauce
10-ounce package frozen
   raspberries

1/6 cup sugar
1/2 tablespoon cornstarch

Thaw and drain raspberries in syrup for raspberry sauce.
Reserve one-half cup syrup. In saucepan, stir together one-
sixth cup sugar and one-half tablespoon cornstarch. Gradually stir in reserved syrup, keeping smooth. Stir in raspberries, cooking over medium heat untill clear, thickened and
boiling. Cool. Store in refrigerator.

Serves: eight to 10.

POACHED PEARS WITH RASPBERRY SAUCE

2 cups water
1/3 cup lemon juice
12 medium-size firm, ripe
   pears
2 cups Chablis or other dry
   white wine
4 cups apple cider
Chocolate Truffle Filling
1 6-ounce package semisweet
   chocolate morsels, melted
1/2 8-ounce package cream
   cheese, melted

1 teaspoon vanilla extract
Raspberry Sauce
2 10-ounce packages frozen
   raspberries in heavy syrup,
   thawed
2/3 cup rose´ wine
1/3 cup raspberry schnapps
   or other raspberry-flavored
   liqueur

Combine two cups water and one-third cup lemon juice; set mixture aside. Cut a thin slice from bottom so pears stand upright. Peel pears using a vegetable peeler; remove core from bottom, cutting to, but not through, the stem end, leaving stems intact. Dip pears in lemon water, coating well. Combine wine and apple cider in a large Dutch oven and bring to a boil. Add pears, standing upright. Cover, reduce heat and simmer 15 to 20 minutes or until pears are tender but still hold their shape. Let cool in cooking liquid then drain.

Combine all ingredients for Chocolate Truffle Filling in a small bowl, stirring until smooth. Fill each cavity with Chocolate Truffle Filling. Chill.

Place raspberries for sauce in container of an electric blender and process until smooth. Pour syrup through a wire-mesh strainer and discard seeds. Combine puree, rose´ wine and raspberry liqueur; chill. To serve, drizzle sauce over pears.

To make ahead, cook pears as directed, and fill with Chocolate Truffle Filling. Make Raspberry Sauce. Refrigerate both eight hours or overnight. Two hours before serving, remove pears from refrigerator to allow chocolate filling to soften. Keep sauce in refrigerator until serving time.
Serves: 12.

*P*EPPERMINT CHOCOLATE DIPPED PRETZELS

1 pound white chocolate   30 pretzel rods
36 unwrapped peppermints

Crush peppermints into small pieces. Melt chocolate on low in double boiler. Line two or three cookie sheets with wax paper. Dip individual rods in melted chocolate. Use a spatula to help smooth on coverage, leaving about an inch or two at top uncovered for handling. Remove from boiler and roll in peppermint pieces. Arrange on lined cookie tins and refrigerate until set.

This is a fun project for two people to make together. Great for mother/daughter gab sessions or afternoon dates on a winter day. These also make tasty gifts when wrapped in cellophane and tied with ribbons.

Yield: two and one-half dozen.

*M*AMIE'S CHOCOLATE CHERRIES

1 pound semi-sweet melting   3 tablespoons light corn
   chocolate   syrup
60 maraschino cherries with   2 cups powdered sugar
   stems
3 tablespoons butter, softened

Drain cherries in colander thoroughly for several hours. Combine butter, syrup and confectioners sugar in mixing bowl, to form a smooth pastry. Shape about one-half tea-spoon of sugar dough around each cherry, leaving only the stem exposed. Place upright on a cookie sheet lined with waxed paper. Put in ice box and chill until set, about three hours. Melt chocolate in double boiler and stir to smooth. Dip chilled cherries thoroughly covering confection. Place cherry stems upright in an air tight container for one to two weeks before serving.

Yield: 60 cherries.

APPLE WALNUT TORTE
With Caramel Rum Sauce

Torte
1 cup unbleached flour
1 cup baking soda
1 teaspoon cinnamon
1/2 teaspoon salt
1 cup sugar
1/4 cup unsalted butter, room
　temperature
1 egg, beaten to blend
1 1/2 cups chopped, peeled
　apples
1/2 cup chopped walnuts

Sauce
1/2 cup whipping cream
1/4 cup unsalted butter
1/2 cup packed dark brown
　sugar
1/2 cup sugar
3 tablespoons dark rum
vanilla ice cream or frozen
　yogurt

Preheat oven at 350°. Butter eight inch diameter cake pan
with two inch high sides. Sift flour, soda, cinnamon and salt
into medium bowl. Using electric mixer, beat sugar and
butter in large bowl until blended. Add egg and beat well.
Stir in dry ingredients, then apples and nuts. Transfer batter
to prepared pan. Bake until tester inserted into center comes
out clean, about 45 minutes. Transfer to rack and cool slightly.
Cover torte.

Combine cream, butter, and sugars for sauce in heavy, medium saucepan over medium heat. Stir until butter melts and
sugar dissolves. Increase heat and boil until slightly thickened, whisking occasionally, about three minutes. Pour sauce
over torte and top with ice cream or frozen yogurt.

Yield: one eight-inch torte.

*E*ASY BUTTER MINTS

1/4 cup butter, softened
1/3 cup light corn syrup
1 teaspoon peppermint
  extract

4 3/4 cups powdered sugar
food coloring

Mix together butter, syrup and peppermint extract. Add powdered sugar, one cup at a time until mixture is well combined or will form a soft ball when rolled in palm of hand. One-quarter teaspoon water may need to be added. Divide dough into as many portions as you want colors. Add one drop of food coloring to each portion. Use two drops if dough is not divided. Shape mixture into one-inch balls and place two inches apart on cookie sheets lined with wax paper. Press flat each ball with textured surface as in fork tines or roll out mixture to one-quarter inch thickness and cut shapes using very small cookie cutters. Let candy dry at room temperature for about three hours. Store in refrigerator for freshness.

Yield: five to six dozen mints.

*C*HRISTMAS BON BONS

14 ounces flaked coconut
4 cups pecans, chopped
1 pound powdered sugar
1/2 cup butter

14 ounces condensed milk
1/4 pound paraffin
12 ounces semi-sweet
  chocolate chips

Mix together coconut, pecans, powdered sugar, butter and milk. Chill one hour. Roll into balls and freeze overnight. Melt paraffin and chocolate in a double boiler. Dip the balls in chocolate with toothpicks. Freeze or keep refrigerated.

Yield: two dozen.

Mom's Hot Fudge Sauce

2 1-ounce squares unsweetened chocolate
1/3 cup of water
1/2 cup sugar

3 tablespoons butter
1/4 teaspoon vanilla
dash salt

Combine chocolate and water and stir over low heat until well blended. Add sugar and salt. Cook slowly, stirring constantly until sugar dissolves and mixture thickens slightly. Add butter and vanilla.

Yield: one cup.

Hot Caramel Sauce

1/2 cup butter
2 cups half and half
1 1/2 cups packed brown
  sugar

1/2 cup sugar
1/8 teaspoon salt
1/8 teaspoon nutmeg
1/8 teaspoon cinnamon

Combine all ingredients and cook over medium heat. Boil about 15 minutes, until thick.

May serve with fruit in fondue or as topping!

Serves: eight.

Riverside Avenue at the bend.
Photograph is from collections at The Riverside/Avondale Preservation Archives.

Side Dishes

Preceding Page: Side Dish from Florida Cracker Party for Boys. For Menu: See Page 229

The giant Treaty Oak and its surrounding acre-age were given as a gift to the city by Jessie Ball duPont. Revered for its natural beauty, the tree is central to much local folklore. Some of the stories may even be true.

Although no known treaty was ever signed under its shade, a newspaper reporter nicknamed this tree the Treaty Oak after World War II.

Photograph is from collections at The Jacksonville Historical Society Archives.

OVEN FRIED GREEN TOMATOES

8 green tomato slices, 1/2 inch thick, unpeeled
butter-flavored cooking spray
1 tablespoon Italian salad dressing

1/2 cup soft bread crumbs
1/8 teaspoon salt
1/8 teaspoon onion powder
1/8 teaspoon pepper

Preheat oven to 400°. Arrange tomato slices on a baking sheet coated with cooking spray; brush dressing on each slice. Combine bread crumbs and remaining ingredients; spoon one tablespoon of crumb mixture on each tomato slice. Spray each slice with cooking spray. Bake for 10 minutes, turn slices over, continue cooking for another eight to 10 minutes.

Serves: four.

SPANISH POTATOES

1 1/4 pounds red-skinned potatoes, scrubbed, halved lengthwise, cut crosswise in one-half inch thick slices and boiled until just tender
1 tablespoon olive oil
1 chicken bouillon cube
1 large onion, coarsely chopped (1 1/2 cups)

1 green bell pepper, diced or substitute 4-ounce can of green chilies
1 - 2 garlic cloves, minced
1 cup picante sauce
1/8 teaspoon dried oregano leaves
1/8 teaspoon pepper

Drain potatoes and leave in colander. In medium saucepan, put one-half cup water, oil and bouillon cube. Bring to a boil, stirring to dissolve bouillon cube. Stir in onion, bell pepper and garlic; return to a boil. Reduce heat to low, cover and simmer 10 minutes, or until vegetables are almost tender. Add tomato, oregano and pepper. Cover and cook three to four minutes, or until vegetables are tender. Add potatoes and cook, stirring gently, until heated through.

Serves: four.

CURRIED ORANGE RICE

1/4 cup butter
1 medium onion, thinly sliced
2 teaspoons curry powder
1 cup uncooked rice
1 cup orange juice

1 cup chicken broth
1 teaspoon salt
1/2 cup seedless raisins
1 bay leaf

Melt butter in heavy saucepan. Saute´ onion until soft and golden but not brown. Stir in curry and rice. Cook two minutes longer, stirring constantly. Add remaining ingredients and stir with fork. Bring to boil then lower heat. Cover and simmer 15 to 20 minutes, or until rice is tender and liquid has been absorbed. Remove bay leaf before serving.

Serves: six.

NEPTUNE NUTTY BANANAS

4 to 6 bananas
1/4 cup honey
1/4 cup lime juice

1 5-ounce can, macadamia
nuts

Peel and slice bananas into one-half inch thick pieces. Coarsely chop macadamia nuts. Dip banana slices in mixture of honey and lime juice. Roll slices in nuts to cover. Refrigerate until serving time.

This is a great accompaniment for pork.

Serves: four.

BROCCOLI SUPREME

2 10-ounce packages chopped
  broccoli
3 cups creamed cottage cheese
3 eggs
6 tablespoons butter, softened,
  divided
1/3 cup flour
1/4 cup finely minced onion
1 can (8 ounces) whole kernel

corn, drained
1/2 pound Cheddar or
  Swiss cheese, diced
1/2 teaspoon salt
1/4 teaspoon pepper
1 - 2 dashes hot pepper
  sauce
2 slices soft bread
1/2 cup crumbled, cooked
  bacon

Heat oven to 350°. Cook broccoli according to package directions and drain. Combine cottage cheese, eggs, four tablespoons butter and flour in blender or mixer bowl. Blend or mix until cottage cheese mixture is smooth and creamy. Fold in broccoli, onion, corn, cheese, salt, pepper and hot pepper sauce. Pour cottage cheese mixture into a greased deep two and one-half quart casserole. Make soft bread crumbs by tearing one bread slice and placing in a blender. Blend until soft crumbs have formed. Repeat with other slice. Melt remaining two tablespoons butter in skillet. Add crumbs and sauté until brown. Sprinkle crumbs and bacon over broccoli mixture. Bake one hour or until mixture is set.

Serves: eight to 10.

My Greek grandmother began preparing dinner each day just after breakfast. She would say, wisely, "You should never wait on dinner, dinner should always wait on you!"

*F*ABULOUS MUSHROOM CASSEROLE

1 pound fresh whole	1/2 cup cream
mushroom caps	1/8 teaspoon salt
1 teaspoon sherry	dash of pepper
1/4 cup butter	1/4 - 1/2 cup bread crumbs
2 beef bouillon cubes	1/2 - 1 cup grated Parmesan
1/2 cup hot water	cheese
2 tablespoons flour	

Preheat oven to 350°. Sauté mushrooms in sherry and butter, reserve liquid. Dissolve beef bouillon cubes in hot water. Blend flour into butter liquid. Add cream, salt, pepper and beef broth. Combine all together. Top with bread crumbs and cheese. Bake uncovered in buttered casserole for 30 minutes.

Serves: four.

*S*OUTHSIDE JOE'S STONE CRAB MUSTARD SAUCE

3 1/2 teaspoons dry mustard	1 teaspoon steak sauce
1 cup mayonnaise	1/8 cup whipping cream
2 teaspoons Worcestershire	1 pinch of salt
sauce	

Mix together with a wire whisk. Serve as a sauce for stone crab.

For a slightly different taste, substitute sour cream for whipping cream.

Yield: one cup.

NANCY'S VEGGIE RELISH

1 16-ounce can white shoepeg corn

1 16-ounce can French cut green beans

1 7-ounce can English peas

1 medium red onion, finely chopped (3 inches in diameter)

1 cup finely chopped celery

1 cup finely chopped green pepper (or 1 4-ounce can chopped mild green chilies, drained)

1 2-ounce jar pimento

Marinade

1 teaspoon salt

1 teaspoon pepper

1/3 cup vegetable oil

1/2 cup plus 1 tablespoon white vinegar

1 cup sugar

1 tablespoon water

Drain corn, green beans and peas. Mix together in a large two quart container. Add onion, celery, green pepper or chilies and pimento then stir. In a separate bowl, mix together marinade ingredients. Pour over vegetable mixture and refrigerate for at least four hours. The longer it marinates, the better it is!

Serves: 8 to 10 as a relish.

Jacksonville Ferry and Land Company, ca. 1921.
Photograph is from the collection of Dr. Wayne Wood.

ASPARAGUS IN SQUASH RINGS

3 pounds fresh asparagus spears

4 to 5 small yellow squash, cut into 1/2 inch thick slices

1/2 cup butter or margarine

1/4 cup lemon juice

1 teaspoon fines herbs*

salt to taste

Snap off tough ends of asparagus. Remove scales from stalks with a knife or vegetable peeler, if desired. Scrape centers from squash slices, leaving one quarter inch flesh with skin. Arrange asparagus in a vegetable steamer over boiling water. Cover and steam three minutes. Add squash to asparagus in steamer. Cover and steam three more minutes or until vegetables are crisp-tender. Add salt to taste. Insert three to four asparagus spears in center of each squash ring. Place on a serving platter and set aside. Combine butter and remaining ingredients in a saucepan. Heat mixture until butter melts. Pour over asparagus.

Fines herbs, a combination of herbs usually including chervil, parsley, chives and tarragon, can be found in the spice section of most supermarkets.

To make ahead: Prepare asparagus and squash for cooking; refrigerate up to eight hours before serving. About 20 to 25 minutes before serving, steam vegetables as directed, make sauce and serve.

Yield: 10 servings.

$\mathscr{P}$ESTO PASTA WITH FETA

2 cups chopped broccoli
1/2 diced sweet red pepper
1/2 cup peas
2 teaspoons sunflower seeds
1/2 teaspoon minced garlic
1 teaspoon Dijon mustard
3 tablespoons low-fat (2%)
  cottage cheese
1/3 cup snipped fresh basil
  leaves

1 tablespoon snipped fresh
  parsley
1 pound pasta spirals,
  cooked according to package directions
2 tablespoons crumbled Feta
  cheese

Steam the broccoli, red pepper and peas until crisp-tender, about five minutes. Rinse immediately under cold water until cool. Place the sunflower seeds, garlic and mustard in a blender or food processor. Puree on medium or high speed until smooth. Add the cottage cheese and blend. Add the basil and parsley, and blend the pesto until smooth. Combine the pasta, broccoli, peppers, peas, pesto and Feta in a serving bowl. Toss until the pesto is evenly distributed. Serve chilled or at room temperature.

Variation: Substitute cauliflower for the peas, and steam one-quarter cup of corn with the broccoli-cauliflower combination. Replace the spirals with medium shells or elbow macaroni.

Pesto can also be spread on toasted peasant bread and covered with sliced tomatoes or put on baked potatoes.

Serves: eight.

$\mathcal{S}$PINACH PESTO

12 ounces rotini pasta
2 cups fresh spinach leaves
1/2 cup olive oil
2 tablespoons chopped
 walnuts

2 garlic cloves, peeled
1/2 teaspoon salt
1/3 cup grated Parmesan
 cheese

Wash and dry spinach leaves. Cook rotini according to package directions. Place spinach, olive oil, walnuts, garlic, salt and Parmesan cheese in food processor and puree at high speed using steel blade. Scrape down sides from time to time. Drain pasta and put in serving bowl. Add sauce and toss to blend.

Pesto will keep in refrigerator for up to two weeks.

Serves: four.

$\mathcal{O}$VEN-FRIED ZUCCHINI CHIPS

3 medium zucchini
1/4 cup frozen egg substitute,
 thawed (or real egg
 equivalent)
2 tablespoons Italian dressing
1/2 cup dry bread crumbs

2 tablespoons grated
 Parmesan cheese
1/8 teaspoon freshly ground
 pepper
vegetable cooking spray

Heat oven to 475°. Cut zucchini into one-quarter inch thick slices; set aside. Combine egg substitute and Italian dressing in a small bowl; stir well. Combine bread crumbs, Parmesan cheese and pepper in a small bowl; stir well. Dip zucchini in egg mixture; dredge in bread crumb mixture. Place zucchini on a baking sheet coated with cooking spray. Bake for five minutes; turn and bake an additional five minutes or until golden. Serve immediately.

Serves: six to eight.

ℬOURBON-LACED SWEET POTATO PUREE

3 pounds sweet potatoes
1/4 cup butter
1/4 cup dark brown sugar, packed
1 tablespoon cornstarch
1 teaspoon salt

3/4 teaspoon cinnamon, ground
1/2 teaspoon nutmeg, grated
1/2 cup milk
1/3 cup bourbon

Preheat oven to 350°. Place the unpeeled sweet potatoes in a large saucepan with enough water to cover and boil until tender, 20 to 25 minutes. When done, remove from the pan and peel while still warm. Place the peeled sweet potatoes in a mixing bowl and mash by hand with a potato masher (do not use a food processor). Add the butter and dry ingredients and mash until smooth then blend the milk and bourbon, making a smooth, moist puree. Transfer to a buttered two quart baking dish. Dot the surface with butter and sprinkle lightly with additional brown sugar. (This may be prepared ahead up to this point. Allow to cool; then cover and refrigerate or freeze.) Bake for about 45 minutes, or until the surface is lightly browned.

Option: Top sweet potatoes with marshmallows before browning, instead of butter and brown sugar.

Serves: 8 to 10.

When my husband and I were still in law school, finals were scheduled for the week after Thanksgiving break. Many students, including ourselves, did not feel they could take the time away from studying to go home for the holiday. Feeling very sorry for ourselves for being denied the traditional get together, we planned a party with some of our close friends. The proviso for coming was to bring whatever dish meant "Thanksgiving Dinner" to them (my husband and I cooked the turkey). We ended up with a smorgasbord of dishes from around the country and sat around the table trying new things, telling stories and Thanksgiving experiences, and forgetting the impending doom of finals week. Even though I always had wonderful Thanksgiving dinners with my family while growing up, when I think of Thanksgiving, I always remember that special one during school when I gave thanks for friends.

*B*AKED POTATOES ON A STICK

16 8-inch bamboo skewers
4 large baking potatoes
1/2 cup olive oil

salt to taste
freshly ground black pepper

Soak bamboo skewers in water for at least three hours. Scrub potatoes thoroughly. Pat dry. Bake in oven at 425° for 35 minutes, or until potatoes are slightly under baked (al dente). Set aside to cool. Cut potatoes in half lengthwise, then again, making four lengthwise quarters. Carefully skewer each piece of potato lengthwise using the bamboo skewers. Lay in a 13-by 9-by 2-inch pan and cover with foil. Chill thoroughly. Transport on ice in a cooler. When ready to grill, brush each potato with a little oil and season with salt and pepper. Grill potatoes on an uncovered grill directly over medium-hot coals for 10 minutes or until lightly browned, turning once.

Perfect for tailgate parties or anytime you grill outdoors!

Yield: 16 pieces or five servings.

*C*RACKER VEGGIES ON A STICK WITH A KICK

8 cherry tomatoes, cut in
   halves
1 green bell pepper, cut into 8
   strips
8 large mushrooms
8 broccoli florets
1 medium onion (3 inches in
   diameter), cut into 8 pieces
Marinade
6 green onions, diced
1 medium onion, diced (3
   inches in diameter)
1 - 2 scotch bonnett or
   jalapeno peppers, seeded
   and minced

3/4 cup low sodium soy
   sauce
1/2 cup red wine vinegar
1/4 cup light olive oil
1/3 cup brown sugar
2 tablespoons chopped fresh
   thyme or 2 teaspoons dried
1/2 teaspoon ground cloves
1/2 teaspoon ground nut-
   meg
1/2 teaspoon allspice or
   cinnamon

Thread veggies on four 10-inch skewers, in the following order: tomato, bell pepper, mushrooms, broccoli, onion. Place in a 9- by 13-inch casserole. Combine marinade ingredients in a food processor for 15 - 20 seconds. Pour over kabobs. Place in refrigerator for at least four hours. Grill for five minutes on each side over medium-hot coals.

Great for grilling and good for you! Variation: add chicken or beef chunks to kabobs and serve over a bed of rice for an entree.

Serves: four.

THANKSGIVING CORNBREAD DRESSING

3 large potatoes (3 1/2 inches in diameter)
2 cups cooked rice
1 package corn muffin mix - cook according to directions
25 saltine crackers, crumbled
1 cup finely chopped onion
3/4 cup finely chopped bell pepper

1 cup finely chopped celery
1/2 teaspoon salt
1/4 teaspoon black pepper
red pepper to taste
2 14-ounce cans of chicken broth

Peel and dice potatoes. Boil until just tender. Mash potatoes with a hand mixer, leaving large and lumpy pieces. Heat oven to 375°. Place potatoes in a large mixing bowl and add cooked rice. Crumble cornbread into large pieces and add to bowl. Add crumbled saltine crackers, onion, bell pepper, celery, salt and peppers to mixture. Add chicken broth to mixture in bowl until very loose and moist (you may not need all of second chicken broth can). Spray a 13- by 9-inch glass cooking dish with vegetable spray. Pour mixture into dish and bake covered for 45 minutes in a 350° oven. Uncover dish and continue baking at 375° for 20 minutes or until golden brown on top.

Serves: eight to 10.

EASY ASPARAGUS CASSEROLE

3 15-ounce cans of asparagus, drained with juice reserved

6 hard boiled eggs, sliced

1 5-ounce jar chopped pimentos

8 ounces extra sharp Cheddar cheese, grated

Sauce

6 tablespoons butter, melted

6 tablespoons flour

3 cups reserved asparagus juice

salt, to taste

pepper, to taste

dash Worchestershire sauce

dash hot pepper sauce

Heat oven to 350°. Spray a 9- by 9-inch baking dish with vegetable spray. Layer asparagus, eggs and pimentos in dish. Combine sauce ingredients and pour sauce on top of layers. Top with cheese. Bake for 40 minutes.

Variations: Substitute one can cream of mushroom soup with two tablespoons of lemon juice for the sauce. Also may add can of sliced mushrooms and green peas. A low calorie topping would be a light layer of bread crumbs.

Serves: six.

MEDITERRANEAN MUSHROOMS

1 tablespoon olive oil

1 - 2 shallots, peeled and minced or 2 tablespoons minced onion

6 garlic cloves, peeled, minced and divided

2 pounds mushrooms, halved or if large, quartered

1 cup dry white wine

1/2 - 3/4 teaspoon dried thyme

1/2 - 3/4 teaspoon dried rosemary

salt to taste

freshly ground black pepper to taste

1/2 cup chopped fresh Italian parsley, divided

In a large heavy skillet, preferably with a nonstick surface, heat the oil over medium-low heat. Add the shallots or onion and half of the garlic. Sauté the vegetables stirring them, until the shallots or onion are tender. Add the mushrooms and the remaining garlic. Sauté the mixture over medium-high heat until the mushrooms start to release their liquid. Add the wine, thyme, rosemary, salt, pepper and half of the parsley. Cook the mixture, stirring it often, over medium heat for 20 minutes or until the mushrooms are tender. Adjust seasonings. Sprinkle the mushrooms with the remaining parsley before serving.

Serve these warm or cold.

Serves: six.

GRATED SWEET POTATO SOUFFLE

2 cups peeled and grated raw
  sweet potatoes
2 eggs, slightly beaten
1/2 cup butter, melted

1/2 cup dark brown sugar
1/4 teaspoon cloves
1/2 teaspoon cinnamon
1/4 teaspoon salt

Heat oven to 350°. Spray a 9- by 9-inch baking dish with vegetable spray. Combine all ingredients and pour into dish. Bake 45 minutes to one hour.

If your family likes very sweet potatoes, you may want to increase brown sugar.

Serves: four.

$\mathscr{E}$ASY SPINACH AND RICE CASSEROLE

1 6-ounce package long -grain and wild rice mix

2 10-ounce packages frozen chopped spinach, thawed

2 cups shredded Monterey Jack cheese

1/4 cup butter or margarine, melted

1 tablespoon chopped onion

3/4 teaspoon dry mustard

1/2 teaspoon salt

Cook rice according to package directions. Dry spinach between paper towels to remove excess moisture. Heat oven to 350°. Combine spinach, rice and remaining ingredients and spoon into a lightly greased two quart shallow casserole. Bake uncovered for 35 - 40 minutes.

Serves: six.

$\mathscr{H}$OLIDAY POTATO CASSEROLE

3 pounds potatoes, peeled and quartered

1/2 cup butter or margarine

6 ounces cream cheese

1 cup shredded cheddar cheese, divided

1 2 -ounce jar diced pimento, drained

1/4 cup milk

1 small green pepper (2 1/2 inches diameter), finely chopped

1 bunch green onions, finely chopped

1/2 cup grated Parmesan cheese

1 teaspoon salt

Cook potatoes in boiling water for 15 minutes or until tender. Drain and mash. Add butter and cream cheese. Beat with electric mixer until smooth. Stir in one-half cup of cheddar cheese and remaining ingredients. Spoon into lightly greased baking dish, (11- by 7 inch or two quart casserole). Cover and chill if desired. Remove from refrigerator at least 30 minutes before baking. Heat oven to 350°. Bake for about 40 minutes until thoroughly heated. Sprinkle with remaining cheddar cheese. Bake for an additional five minutes to melt cheese.

Serves: 8 to 10.

$\mathscr{F}$LORIDA-GEORGIA GRITS CASSEROLE

1 quart milk	1/4 cup grated Parmesan
1/2 cup butter	cheese
1 teaspoon salt	paprika
1 cup regular grits	
1 whole wheel Gruyere	
cheese, grated	

Heat oven to 350°. Bring milk, one-half stick of butter and salt to boil. Sprinkle in grits, stirring constantly. Cover and lower heat. Cook until consistency is like mush, not too thick and dry, about 10 - 15 minutes. Put in mixer and beat five minutes. Pour in flat buttered casserole dish, (9- by 9-inch or 11- by 9-inch), and let it sit about 15 minutes. Make crisscross marks with knife, close together. Pour one-half stick melted butter all over, making sure it goes down into casserole. Sprinkle coarsely grated Gruyere on top, then Parmesan followed by sprinkling of paprika. Bake for 30 minutes.

This can be made ahead of time or the night before.

Serves: six to eight.

$\mathscr{C}$URRANT - JALAPENO PEPPER JELLY

4 12-ounce jars red currant	1/4 cup white vinegar
jelly	
1/3 cup seeded, diced	
jalapeno pepper	

Melt jelly in a heavy saucepan over low heat. Add pepper and vinegar. Bring to a boil, reduce heat, and simmer five minutes. Skim off foam with a metal spoon. Quickly pour into hot sterilized jars, filling to one-half inch from top; wipe jar rims. Cover with metal lids, and screw on bands. Refrigerate up to three months.

An easy to make gift! Serve with turkey, ham, pork or cream cheese and crackers.

Yield: eight half-pints.

CRANBERRY SAUSAGE TARTLETTES

1 1/2 cup whole cranberries, fresh or frozen
1/2 cup sugar
1/2 cup orange juice
1 pound fresh Italian sausage, remove from casings
1 cup minced green onions

salt to taste
freshly ground black pepper to taste
4 - 8 regular size tartlette shells (four inches diameter) recipe follows

Combine cranberries, sugar and juice in a saucepan. Bring to a boil; simmer until cranberries are soft and some have popped their skins, about 20 minutes. Remove from heat and set aside. In a nonstick skillet, sauté crumbled sausage. Drain well on paper towels and return sausage to skillet. Add green onions to sausage and cook over medium-low heat for two minutes. Add salt and pepper to taste. Mix cranberry and sausage mixtures, heat and fill shells.

Tartlette Pastry
2 cups flour
1 teaspoon salt
12 tablespoons unsalted butter, chilled

2 tablespoons vegetable shortening, chilled
6 - 8 tablespoons ice water

Heat oven to 350°. Mix flour and salt in a large bowl. Cut in butter and shortening. Work dough until it resembles cornmeal. Add iced water, one tablespoon at a time, until dough begins to hold a shape. Roll into a ball, refrigerate one hour. Roll out thinly and line one and one-half inch diameter tartlette tins with pastry. Cover and place tins in freezer until ready to bake. Bake until lightly colored, about 15 minutes. If crusts puff up while baking pierce immediately with a fork. Cool and store in an airtight container for up to two days.

In a hurry? Use ready made pie crust, roll out and line your tartlette tins.

Yield: four to eight tartlettes.

ORZO WITH GARLIC AND PARMESAN CHEESE

6 cups water
salt to taste
1 cup orzo (rice shaped pasta)
2 tablespoons olive oil
1 tablespoon butter
1 teaspoon finely chopped
  garlic
1/2 teaspoon grated orange
  rind

1/4 teaspoon red pepper
  flakes, optional
4 tablespoons finely chopped
  Italian parsley
4 tablespoons grated
  Parmesan cheese
freshly ground black pepper
  to taste

Bring the water to a boil in a saucepan and add salt. Add the orzo. Cook, stirring about 10 minutes or until tender. Do not overcook. Reserve one-quarter cup of the cooking liquid. Drain the orzo. Heat the oil and butter in a saucepan. Add the garlic and cook briefly, stirring. Do not brown. Add the drained orzo, orange rind, pepper flakes, reserved cooking liquid, parsley, cheese and pepper. Toss well and serve immediately.

Serves: four.

ORZO FLORENTINE

2 teaspoons margarine or
  butter
2 cloves garlic, minced
3 1/2 cups water
1 1/2 cups orzo (rice shaped
  pasta)
1/4 teaspoon salt

2 cups tightly packed, fresh
  chopped spinach
4 tablespoons freshly grated
  Parmesan cheese
2 tablespoons toasted pine
  nuts

Melt margarine or butter in medium saucepan. Add garlic and sauté for one minute. Add water, orzo, and salt and bring to a boil. Reduce heat to medium-low and cook 12 minutes or until liquid is absorbed. Stir in spinach, cheese and pine nuts. Serve immediately.

Serves: four.

CARRIBEAN CARROTS

2 tablespoons margarine
1 cup unsweetened pineapple
   juice
1 tablespoon chopped ginger
3 tablespoons brown sugar
1/2 teaspoon ground nutmeg
1/2 teaspoon ground ginger
1/2 teaspoon red pepper
   flakes
salt to taste
freshly ground black pepper

3 - 4 cups sliced carrots
   (about 3 - 4 large carrots)
1 red onion (3 inches
   diameter), peeled and
   thinly sliced
1 cup fresh pineapple chunks
3 tablespoons chopped
   parsley, divided in half
3 tablespoons chopped mint,
   divided in half

Melt the margarine in a large three quart Dutch oven over
medium heat. Add the pineapple juice, chopped ginger,
brown sugar, nutmeg, ground ginger, red pepper flakes, salt
and pepper to taste. Bring to a boil and stir in the carrots and
onion. Cover, reduce the heat to a simmer, and cook for six
minutes. Add the pineapple chunks, one and one-half tablespoon of the parsley and one and one-half tablespoon of the
mint and continue cooking, uncovered, until the carrots are
crisp and tender and most of the liquid has cooked away,
about six to eight minutes longer. Transfer to a serving bowl
with a slotted spoon and garnish with the remaining parsley
and mint.

Serves: eight.

CREAMY LIMA BEANS

1 cup water
1 16-ounce package frozen
   Fordhook lima beans

3/4 cup whipping cream
freshly ground black pepper
1 tablespoon butter

Bring water to a boil in a medium saucepan. Add lima beans,
bring to second boil and simmer 10 minutes. Drain beans and
add remaining ingredients, mix well and serve.

Serves: four.

SWEET-POTATO FLOWERS

3 pounds sweet potatoes
1/4 cup melted butter or
  margarine
1/4 cup maple flavored syrup
1 4-ounce can pineapple
  tidbits

optional: 1/4 cup fresh
  cranberries, for center of
  flower

Peel sweet potatoes and cut into paper thin (one-eighth inch thick) crosswise slices. Put potatoes in a large saucepan with water just to cover; bring to a boil. Reduce heat, cover and simmer eight to 10 minutes until crisp-tender; drain. Rinse with cold water; drain again. Lightly grease eight, one-half cup ramekins or disposable aluminum-foil baking cups. Starting from the outside and working toward center of cup, arrange potato slices slightly overlapping like petals of a flower. For center, roll up one long potato slice. (Can be prepared ahead to this point. Wrap well and refrigerate.) Preheat oven to 400°. To complete, sprinkle with crushed pineapple. Arrange flowers in a shallow baking pan. Drizzle some melted butter over each; brush edges with syrup. Bake 20 minutes or until lightly browned on edges.

These sweet potatoes are beautiful! Easily assembled the day before and baked while the turkey sits waiting to be carved.

Serves: eight.

GRANDMA'S HERBED GREEN BEANS

2 pounds fresh green beans
1 small onion (2 inches in
diameter), sliced
2 cloves garlic, minced
1 tablespoon olive oil
3/4 cup water

1/2 teaspoon sugar
1/2 teaspoon salt
1/2 teaspoon pepper
1/4 teaspoon dried whole
tarragon

Wash beans and remove strings. Leave whole or cut in half, if desired. Sauté onion and garlic in oil in a Dutch oven. Add beans, water and remaining ingredients. Bring to a boil, cover, reduce heat and simmer 20 minutes or until tender. Add additional water if necessary.

Beans may be cooked a day ahead and reheated.

Serves: eight.

GREEN BEANS IN MUSTARD SAUCE

1 one-pound package frozen
green beans or one and
one-half pounds fresh
2 ounces butter
1/4 cup chopped green
onions
1 clove garlic, minced
1/3 cup whipping cream
1 tablespoon yellow mustard

1 tablespoon brown or gourmet mustard
1/2 teaspoon salt
1/2 teaspoon sugar
1/4 teaspoon pepper
1 2-ounce jar chopped
pimentos, drained

Steam green beans for eight to 10 minutes. Drain and set aside. In a medium saucepan melt butter. Sauté green onion and garlic for two minutes. Remove from heat. Add whipping cream, mustards, salt, sugar and pepper; stir well. Heat sauce slowly and add green beans, heating thoroughly. Add drained pimentos. Garnish with dark tops of green onions. Stir and serve immediately.

Serves: six.

ASPARAGUS WITH WARM TOMATO VINAIGRETTE

3 cups of water
1/2 teaspoon salt
1 pound of fresh asparagus
3 tablespoons olive oil
1 1/2 tablespoon tarragon
  white wine vinegar
1/2 teaspoon honey

2 ripe medium tomatoes
1/2 teaspoon dried whole
  oregano
1/2 teaspoon dried whole
  thyme
salt to taste
freshly ground black pepper

Wash and trim ends of asparagus. Peel lower half of spears with vegetable peeler if desired. Boil water and salt in a large skillet over high heat. Add asparagus to boiling water. Cover and cook three to five minutes until spears are tender but not soft. Wash, seed and chop tomatoes; set aside. Heat olive oil over medium heat in a small saucepan. Stir in vinegar, honey, tomatoes and spices. Heat through (about three minutes). Drain asparagus and arrange on a platter. Pour sauce over asparagus. Serve warm or at room temperature.

Serves: four.

Volunteer Lifeguards at Jacksonville Beach Red Cross Life Saving Corps Station. Photograph is from collections at The Beaches Area Historical Society Archives.

$\mathcal{L}$OWFAT GREEN RICE

2 large poblano chiles
2 cloves garlic, finely chopped
1 medium onion (about 1/2 cup), chopped

1 cup uncooked regular rice
2 cups chicken broth
1/4 teaspoon salt
1/4 cup snipped parsley

Roast, peel and seed chiles. Place chilies, garlic and onion in food processor. Process until smooth. Mix chile mixture and remaining ingredients except parsley in three quart saucepan. Heat to boiling, stirring once or twice; reduce heat. Cover and simmer 16 minutes. Do not lift cover or stir. Remove from heat; fluff rice lightly with fork. Cover and let steam 10 minutes. Stir in parsley.

Serves: six.

$\mathcal{G}$OURMET WILD RICE

1/3 cup currants
2 tablespoons brandy
2/3 cup wild rice

2 cups chicken broth
2 tablespoons olive oil
1/3 cup toasted pine nuts

Combine currants and brandy then set aside. Wash wild rice in three changes of hot water, drain. Combine wild rice and chicken broth in a medium saucepan. Bring to a boil. Cover, reduce heat and simmer 45 minutes or until rice is tender and liquid is absorbed. Stir in currant mixture, olive oil and pine nuts.

Serves: six.

$\mathcal{T}$ARRAGON RICE

1 medium onion, chopped
1/2 cup melted butter
1 cup uncooked rice

2 cups chicken broth
1 1/2 tablespoon tarragon

Melt butter in a medium saucepan and stir in onion. Sauté onion until translucent. Add rice and stir until it begins to brown. Add tarragon and stir. Bring two cups of chicken broth to boil in a separate saucepan. Add rice mixture to broth, simmer for 20 minutes. Stir again before serving.

Serves: four to six.

*B*AKED VIDALIA SWEET ONIONS

4 large Vidalia onions   4 tablespoons butter
salt and pepper

Heat oven to 350°. Core a large Vidalia onion. Sprinkle with salt and pepper. Place one tablespoon of butter into the hollow of each onion. Wrap individually in foil and bake for 30 to 40 minutes depending on size of onion.

Serves: four.

Known as the sweetest onion in the world, the Vidalia onion is a local favorite and is readily available during the summer months.

*R*ACHEL'S ONION SQUARES

2 eggs, one beaten   3/4 cup sour cream
3/4 cup milk   1/2 teaspoon salt
2 cups biscuit baking mix   1/4 teaspoon freshly ground
2 tablespoons poppy seeds   black pepper
2 cups chopped Vidalia onion paprika
2 tablespoons butter

Heat oven to 400°. Blend beaten egg and milk with biscuit baking mix and poppy seeds. Turn into a greased 9- by 9-inch pan. Sauté onions in butter until tender and light brown. Spread on dough. Beat remaining egg with sour cream and season with salt and pepper. Spread over onions. Bake for 25 minutes. Cool slightly and cut into squares and sprinkle with paprika.

Serves: six.

*D*OUG'S DEEP DISH VIDALIAS

2 cups water
1 cup uncooked long-grain
  rice
6 large Vidalia onions
  (4 inches in diameter)
1/2 cup butter or margarine
2 tablespoons minced fresh
  parsley

1/4 teaspoon salt
1/4 teaspoon white pepper
1 cup (4 ounces) shredded
  Swiss cheese
1 cup whipping cream
paprika

Heat oven to 350°. Bring water to a boil in a medium sauce-pan. Add rice. Cover, reduce heat and simmer 10 minutes. Drain and set aside. Peel and chop onions. Melt butter in a Dutch oven over medium heat. Add onion and cook for 15 minutes, stirring frequently. Remove from heat, stir in rice, parsley, salt, pepper, cheese and cream. Spoon mixture into a lightly greased 13- by 9- by 2-inch baking dish. Cover and bake for 30 minutes. Sprinkle lightly with paprika before serving.

Serves: 8 to10.

View of pavillion on Jacksonville Beach taken in 1945.
Photograph is from collections at The Beaches Area Historical Society Archives.

COASTAL CORN DRESSING

4 ounces butter
1 large green bell pepper (3 1/2 inches in diameter), or use 2 small ones
1 large red or yellow bell pepper (3 1/2 inches in diameter) or 2 small ones
2 cloves garlic, finely chopped
2 leeks, finely chopped
2 15-ounce cans whole corn with juice
1 17-ounce can cream style corn
3 cups corn bread stuffing or dry homemade stuffing, reserve 1/2 cup
1 tablespoon crumbled sage
1 1/2 teaspoons salt
1/2 teaspoon pepper
10 ounces sharp cheddar cheese, grated
16 ounces sour cream
3 large eggs

Heat oven to 350°. Spray a large saucepan with vegetable cooking spray. Finely chop bell peppers. Melt butter in saucepan. Add green and red or yellow bell pepper and garlic. Saute´ for two minutes. Add leeks to pot and saute´ for an additional two minutes. Remove from heat. Add whole and cream style corn, two and one-half cups stuffing, sage, salt, pepper and grated cheese to pot. Mix well. Blend sour cream and eggs together using blender or hand mixer. Add to corn-stuffing mixture. Spray a two and one-half quart Pyrex baking dish with vegetable cooking spray or grease with butter. Coat sides of dish with one-half cup stuffing. Pour corn-stuffing mixture into dish. Bake for one hour and 40 minutes. Cover with foil if top starts to get too brown after an hour of cooking.

Can be prepared in advance and cooked before serving, remember to let it sit for at least an hour before going from refrigerator to oven. Add ham or turkey chunks, (at least one and one-half cups), for a full meal casserole.

Serves: 8 to 10.

GLAZED RED CABBAGE

4 ounces butter, divided
5 ounces seedless raspberry
jam, reserve 1 tablespoon
1/2 cup red wine or black-
berry wine

1 teaspoon salt
3 tablespoons apple cider
vinegar
2 pounds red cabbage, hand
chopped

Melt two ounces butter in a medium saucepan. Add raspberry jam, wine, salt, and vinegar. Mix well. Bring mixture to
a boil and add cabbage. Reduce heat to low. Cook for one and
one-half to two hours, stirring occasionally. Cook mixture
down until approximately one-third of liquid remains. Thirty
minutes before serving, cook mixture down dry and add two
ounces butter and remaining one tablespoon raspberry jam.
Serve immediately.

Serves: six to eight.

T.P.C. MASHED POTATOES
(Terry's Perfect Celery Mashed Potatoes)

6 large potatoes, peeled and
cubed
2 ounces butter
5 celery stalks, thinly sliced
1 carrot, chopped
2 onions, chopped

2-3 cloves garlic, minced
1 1/2 cups half-and-half or
milk
1 1/2 teaspoons salt
1/2 teaspoon pepper

Cook potatoes in a large pot of boiling water until tender.
Drain well. Set aside. Melt butter in a large saucepan. Add
celery, carrot, onion and garlic. Saute´ until tender-crisp,
approximately four to five minutes. Add half-and-half, salt
and pepper to vegetable mixture. Heat to boiling, stirring
constantly. Add potatoes, heat briefly and remove from heat.
Mash mixture using electric hand mixer.

Serves: 8 to 10.

$\mathscr{L}$INDA'S BROCCOLI CASSEROLE

2 10-ounce packages frozen
  chopped broccoli
1/4 cup chopped onion
1 cup water
1/2 cup grated cheese (your
  choice)

1 cup mayonnaise
1 cup canned cream of
  mushroom soup
2 eggs
salt and pepper to taste
1/2 cup bread crumbs

Heat oven to 350°. Place broccoli, onion and water in a medium saucepan. Cook according to package instructions, drain and cool. Mix grated cheese, mayonnaise, mushroom soup and eggs together in a medium bowl. Add cooked broccoli. Mix well and add salt and pepper to taste. Pour into a greased one and one-half quart casserole. Bake for 40 minutes. Cover with bread crumbs and bake for an additional 10 minutes.

Serves: six.

$\mathscr{M}$OLLY'S FAT FREE SAUCE

for Seafood and Veggies

2 cups fat-free mayonnaise
2 tablespoons hot Chinese
  yellow mustard

1/2 cup mango chutney or
  apricot preserves

Mix all ingredients together. Taste, adjust mustard and serve. This is excellent on steamed vegetables and broiled fish.

Variation: Using same mayonnaise base; add a few minced shallots, lemon juice, drop or two of hot pepper sauce and dill — for a great spread for baked potatoes or sauce for fish.

Yield: two and one-half cups.

Little Chester, 1927.

Entrees

Preceding Page: Entree from A Southern Game Supper.
For Menu: See Page 238

Plantation homes are still a very popular style in this region. Their inviting porches and high ceilings give relief from the hot summer climate.

Feeding Ostriches, Jacksonville, Fla.

While the abundance of wild game kept local hunters busy, ostrich farms were at one time a popular enterprise, being prized for their eggs and plumage.

Photograph is from collections at The Beaches Area Historical Society.

TANGY SHRIMP KABOBS

1/3 cup lemon juice
1 tablespoon ground mustard
1 tablespoon vegetable oil
1 teaspoon ground cumin
1/2 teaspoon ground
 coriander
1/2 teaspoon salt

1/8 teaspoon paprika
1 1/2 pounds fresh raw
 large shrimp, peeled
 and deveined
2 limes
3 cups hot cooked rice, if
 desired

Mix all ingredients except shrimp, limes and rice in shallow glass or plastic dish. Add shrimp and turn shrimp to coat with marinade. Cover and refrigerate one hour. Remove shrimp from marinade; reserve marinade. Cut limes into one-half inch slices; cut slices into fourths. Thread shrimp and lime pieces alternately on each of six 15-inch metal skewers, leaving space between each. Cover with grill lid and grill kabob five to six inches from medium coals six to 10 minutes, turning and brushing two or three times with marinade, until shrimp are pink. Serve over rice. Discard any remaining marinade.

Serves: six.

"My grandfather always infuriated the cook by saying upon the completion of each meal, "I don't know if that was good or if I was just hungry."

$\mathscr{B}$UTTERFLIED COCONUT SHRIMP

1 pound large shrimp,
   shelled and deveined
oil
1/4 cup flour
1/2 teaspoon salt
1/2 teaspoon dry mustard

1 egg
2 tablespoons cream of coconut or whipping cream
3/4 cup flaked coconut
1/2 cup bread crumbs

Slit shrimp along curved side, cutting almost through. Place on paper towel. Heat two inches of oil in saucepan to 350°. Combine flour, salt and dry mustard in a small bowl. Beat egg and cream of coconut in small bowl. In third bowl, combine coconut and bread crumbs. Dip shrimp in flour mixture, then in egg mixture, then in coconut mixture. Refrigerate until ready to cook. When oil is hot, fry shrimp a few at a time for two minutes or until golden, turning once. Remove with slotted spoon and drain on paper towel. Keep warm in oven.

Yield: Serves four.

$\mathscr{C}$REAMED SHRIMP IN CHIPOTLE SAUCE

1 pound medium shrimp
4 tablespoons oil
1/4 cup chopped onion
1/2 cup finely chopped,
   peeled ripe tomatoes
1/2 cup heavy cream

1 cup mayonnaise
1 teaspoon pickling sauce
   from a can of chipotle chiles
Salt and pepper
1 teaspoon ground cumin

Peel and devein shrimp. Heat two tablespoons oil in wok or large skillet or dutch oven and stir-fry three minutes. Add two tablespoons oil, onion and tomatoes and stir-fry two more minutes. Add cream. Mix mayonnaise with chipotle sauce and add to cooked shrimp. Sprinkle with cumin. Taste for seasoning. Serve over steamed white rice, buttered pasta or buttered, toasted English muffins.

Serves: four.

JAZZ FEST CREOLE

2 pounds shrimp, cooked
1/2 cup finely chopped green
 pepper
2/3 cup shortening
1/2 cup flour
2 cups hot water
4 whole bay leaves
1 cup chopped green onions
 and tops
1 teaspoon crushed thyme
dash cayenne pepper

6-8 crushed garlic cloves
3 teaspoons salt
2 8-ounce cans tomato sauce
1 can tomatoes (halves or
 chopped)
1 cup chopped parsley tops
2 lemon slices
1 16-ounce package
 commercial saffron rice
 mix, cooked according to
 directions

Small shrimp are tastier, but if large ones are used, cut in half. Melt shortening; blend in flour-stirring constantly. Add remaining ingredients (except rice), cover, and simmer 20 minutes. You may simmer longer. If you do, don't add cooked shrimp until the final 20 minutes. Remove bay leaves and lemon slices. Serve over hot rice and garnish with extra parsley.

Serves: eight.

A Boy and his Large Mouth Black Bass, Southpoint Area.

ATLANTIC BEACH SHRIMP BAKE

2 pounds fresh shrimp, cooked
1 4-ounce can mushrooms
1/2 chopped green pepper
1/2 cup chopped onion
1/2 cup chopped pimento
1 cup chopped celery
1 cup mayonnaise
1/2 teaspoon salt
1/8 teaspoon pepper
1 cup cream
1 tablespoon Worcestershire sauce
1/2 cup cooked rice
bread crumbs

Preheat oven to 375°. Mix all ingredients except bread-crumbs and place in a two quart buttered casserole. Sprinkle with bread crumbs and bake for 30 minutes.

Serve in pastry shells for an elegant lunch.

Serves: six.

ANGEL HAIR PASTA
With Sundried Tomatoes, Lemon and Seafood

1 pound angel hair pasta
3 tablespoons olive oil
4 tablespoons unsalted butter
6 cloves garlic, chopped
1/2 pound medium shrimp, uncooked, peeled and deveined
1/2 pound sea scallops
1 bottle clam juice
1/2 cup oil-packed sun-dried tomatoes, drained and chopped
1/2 cup parsley, chopped
peel from one lemon, removed in strips and cut julienne

Cook pasta al dente; drain. Toss with one tablespoon olive oil. Set aside. Melt butter and two tablespoons olive oil in a heavy, large skillet over low heat. Add garlic and sauté until tender, about three minutes. Increase heat to medium-high. Add shrimp and scallops. Sauté until pink, about two minutes. Add clam juice and pasta to skillet. Increase heat to high and cook until pasta absorbs most of liquid and mixture is heated through, tossing about five minutes. Add tomatoes, parsley and lemon to pasta and toss gently. Serve immediately.

Serves: four to five.

NEPTUNE BEACH CRAB CAKES

1/4 cup butter or margarine, melted
1/4 cup finely chopped onion
2 tablespoons chopped green pepper
1 pound fresh crabmeat
1 to 1 1/4 cups fine dry bread crumbs
1 large egg, lightly beaten
1 tablespoon mayonnaise

1 tablespoon dried parsley flakes
1 tablespoon lemon juice
1 teaspoon Worcestershire sauce
1 teaspoon seafood seasoning
1 teaspoon dry mustard
dash ground red pepper
vegetable oil

Melt butter in large skillet over medium heat. Add onion and green pepper and cook, stirring constantly until tender. Remove from heat. Stir in crabmeat, three-quarters cup bread crumbs, egg, mayonnaise, parsley, lemon juice, Worcestershire, seafood seasoning, dry mustard, and red pepper. Shape mixture into eight patties and coat with remaining bread crumbs. Pour oil to depth of one-quarter inch into a large heavy skillet. Fry patties in hot oil over medium heat, four to five minutes on each side.

Serves: four.

"My brother-in-law will long be remembered as a tremendous help in the kitchen. When he was five years old, living in Baltimore, he accompanied his mother who was preparing fresh crab for supper. Somehow the crabs got out and ended up on the kitchen floor. His mother, being barefoot at the time, found herself held hostage in the dark by her son who turned off the lights to add to the hilarity."

$\mathcal{T}$RICOLOR PASTA WITH CLAM SAUCE

6 6 1/2-ounce cans chopped
  clams, undrained
2 tablespoons butter or
  margarine
1 1/2 tablespoons olive oil
1/4 cup finely chopped
  onion
4 cloves garlic, minced
1/2 cup Chablis or other
  dry white wine
1/4 cup chopped fresh
  parsley
1 tablespoon spaghetti
  seasoning mix
1 tablespoon dried Italian
  seasoning
2 tablespoons lemon juice
1 8-ounce package squid ink
  flavored angel hair pasta
1 8-ounce package tomato
  flavored angel hair pasta
1 8-ounce package spinach
  flavored angel hair pasta
2 tablespoons grated
  Parmesan cheese

Drain clams, reserving one cup liquid; set aside. Melt butter in a large skillet. Add olive oil, onion and garlic. Cook over medium heat, stirring constantly, until tender. Stir in wine and cook, stirring occasionally, until liquid is reduced to one-quarter cup. Add clam, and reserved liquid, parsley, spaghetti seasoning, Italian seasoning and lemon juice. Cook, stirring occasionally, about 30 minutes, or until mixture is of sauce consistency. Combine pastas, and cook according to package directions, drain. Transfer to a large serving platter, spoon clam sauce over pasta and sprinkle with Parmesan cheese.

You may substitute eight ounces of regular angel hair pasta for any of the three kinds of flavored pasta.

Serves: 10 to 12.

$\mathcal{S}$EASIDE ENCHILADAS

6 soft shell tortillas
1 cup sour cream
1/2 cup salsa
6 - 8 ounces shredded
  Monterey Jack cheese
1/4 cup chopped green
  onions

1/4 cup cottage cheese
1/2 pound shrimp, shelled
   and deveined
1/2 pound scallops

black olives
5 tablespoons milk
Parmesan cheese

Preheat oven to 350°. Mix sour cream and salsa in bowl and set aside. Place shells out flat and spoon three to four tablespoons of sour cream mixture on each shell. Place shrimp and scallops straight across middle of shell. Sprinkle three to four tablespoons of shredded cheese over seafood and roll up. Place seam side down into lightly greased 13- by 9-inch baking dish. In food processor, blend cottage cheese, milk and Parmesan. Pour over tortillas and sprinkle with green onions and black olives. Bake for 30 minutes.

Serves: four to six.

AUNT ZO'S CRAB "SHALA"

2 onions, chopped
2 bell peppers, chopped
1/2 cup olive oil
3 8-ounce cans of tomato
   sauce or 2 15-ounce cans
   whole tomatoes, cut through
2 sticks celery, chopped

3 small bay leaves
1 teaspoon oregano
salt and pepper to taste
18 small crabs, cleaned and
   steamed, but not shelled
   or 1 pound crabmeat

Puree chopped onions and pepper in blender or food processor. Heat olive oil and sauté chopped celery. Do not drain oil. Add all ingredients, except crabs, in large dutch oven or sauce pot and cook for 30 minutes. Add crabs. Simmer 10 minutes more. Remove bay leaves. Serve over cooked spaghetti.

This dish is intended to be served with the crabs in the shells. It's messy, but delicious!

Serves: six.

$\mathcal{S}$ALMON LOAF
With Creamy Dill Sauce

6 tablespoons salad oil
2 cups finely chopped celery
1 1/2 cups chopped onion
3 7 3/4-ounce cans salmon
3 large eggs
1 12-ounce can evaporated milk
3 cups fresh bread crumbs
3 teaspoons salt
1 teaspoon pepper

Dill Sauce
1 1/2 cups mayonnaise
3/4 cup sour cream
3 tablespoons lemon juice
3 tablespoons milk
2 teaspoons finely chopped dill or 1 1/2 teaspoons dried dillweed
1 teaspoon salt
1 1/2 teaspoons sugar
1/4 teaspoon pepper

About one and one-half hours before serving or day ahead, in a two-quart saucepan over medium-high heat, cook celery and onion in salad oil until tender, about 10 minutes. Remove saucepan from heat. Add salmon with its liquid and remaining ingredients except dill sauce. With fork or pastry blender, combine mixture until well mixed and smooth. Preheat oven to 350°. Grease large loaf pan. Spoon salmon mixture evenly into pan. Bake loaf 60 minutes or until knife inserted in center comes out clean. Remove loaf from pan. Serve hot or cold with dill sauce.

Serves: eight.

$\mathcal{G}$RILLED FISH WITH MELON-JICAMA SALSA

1 1/2 pounds swordfish, tuna or marlin steaks, 3/4 to 1 inch thick
3 tablespoons olive or vegetable oil
1 tablespoon lime juice
1/4 teaspoon salt
1/8 teaspoon crushed red pepper

Salsa
1 cup chopped cantaloupe
1 cup chopped honey dew melon
1/2 cup chopped jicama
2 tablespoons sliced green onions
2 tablespoons chopped fresh cilantro

1 tablespoon finely chopped
  ginger root
2 tablespoons lime juice

1 jalapeno pepper, seeded
  and finely chopped

If fish steaks are large, cut into six serving pieces. Mix oil, lime juice, salt and red pepper in shallow glass or plastic dish. Add fish; turn to coat with marinade. Cover and refrigerate 30 minutes. Remove fish from marinade; reserve marinade. Cover and grill fish five to six minutes, brushing two or three times with marinade and turning once, until fish flakes easily with fork. Discard any remaining marinade. Serve fish with Melon-Jicama Salsa. Garnish with lime wedges if desired.

Serves: six.

$\mathcal{M}$ACADAMIA MAHI-MAHI

2 pounds mahi-mahi fillets
1/2 teaspoon salt
1/8 teaspoon pepper
2 tablespoons butter or
  margarine
2 tablespoons lemon juice

1/4 cup butter or
  margarine
1 cup chopped
  macadamia nuts
1 tablespoon chopped
  fresh parsley

Cut fish into serving-size portions. Sprinkle with salt and pepper; place fillets on rack of a well-greased broiler pan. Set aside. Combine two tablespoons butter and lemon juice; brush over fish, reserving remaining mixture for basting. Broil five to six inches from heat (with electric oven door partially opened) five minutes. Turn fish; baste with remaining lemon juice mixture. Broil four to five additional minutes or until fish flakes easily when tested with a fork. Transfer to serving platter. Melt one-quarter cup butter in skillet over medium heat. Add macadamia nuts and cook, stirring constantly, until lightly browned. Remove from heat and add parsley. Pour over fish. Serve immediately.

Serves: six.

SPICY SNAPPER SAN MARCO

2 medium onions, cut into
  1/2 inch slices
1 sweet red pepper, cut into
  rings
1 or 2 jalapeno peppers,
  seeded and cut into thin
  strips

2 tablespoons vegetable oil
1/4 cup rice vinegar
1/4 to 1/2 teaspoon oregano
6 red snapper fillets (about 2
  pounds)
1/2 teaspoon pepper

Preheat oven to 350°. Cook onions and two kinds of peppers in oil in a skillet over medium heat about five minutes, stirring constantly. Add vinegar and oregano. Cook one minute and set aside. Sprinkle red snapper fillets with pepper; place, skin side down, in a single layer in a lightly greased 15- by 10-by 1-inch jellyroll pan. Bake at 350° for 15 minutes. Spoon onion mixture over fish, and bake five additional minutes or until fish flakes easily when tested with a fork.

Serves: six.

CHEESY FISH FILLETS WITH SPINACH

2 tablespoons butter
2 tablespoons flour
1 teaspoon instant chicken
  bouillon
dash nutmeg
dash cayenne pepper
dash white pepper
1 cup milk
2/3 cup shredded Swiss or
  Cheddar cheese

1 10-ounce package frozen
  chopped spinach, thawed
  and well drained
1 tablespoon lemon juice
1 pound fish fillets, cut into
  serving pieces
1 teaspoon salt
2 tablespoons grated
  Parmesan cheese
paprika

Heat oven to 350°. Heat butter over low heat until melted. Stir in flour, bouillon, nutmeg, cayenne pepper and white pepper; cook over low heat, stirring constantly until mixture in smooth and bubbly. Stir in milk; heat to boiling and cook, stirring constantly for one minute. Add cheese and cook, stirring constantly, just until cheese melts. Set aside. Place spinach in ungreased 12- by 7 1/2-inch baking dish or eight-inch square baking dish. Sprinkle with the lemon juice. Arrange fish on spinach; sprinkle with salt. Spread sauce over fish and spinach. Bake uncovered until fish flakes easily with a fork, about 20 minutes. Sprinkle with the Parmesan cheese and paprika; return to oven for five minutes.

Serves: four.

ORANGE GINGER MARINATED SWORDFISH STEAKS

10 8-ounce swordfish steaks, about 1 inch thick
1 1/2 cups tomato-based barbecue sauce
1 cup white wine
2 tablespoons grated orange rind
1 cup orange juice

1/4 cup soy sauce
2 tablespoons finely chopped fresh ginger root
4 cloves garlic, minced
vegetable cooking spray
garnishes: parsley sprigs, orange slices

Arrange fish in a large shallow dish. Combine barbecue sauce, wine, orange rind, orange juice, soy sauce, ginger root and garlic then pour over fish. Cover and refrigerate two to 24 hours, turning occasionally. Remove fish from marinade, discarding marinade. Place fish in grill baskets that have been coated with cooking spray. Cook, covered with grill lid, over medium coals (300° - 350°), 10 minutes on each side. Garnish, if desired, and serve immediately.

Serves: 10.

CHICKEN DELIGHT

1 whole chicken or 8 to 9
  boneless, skinless chicken
  breasts
6 medium potatoes
1 cup vegetable oil
1/2 cup vinegar
1 10 3/4-ounce can cream of
  mushroom soup
1/2 teaspoon paprika

1/2 teaspoon parsley
  flakes
1 medium onion, sliced
1 tablespoon salt
1/2 teaspoon pepper
1/2 teaspoon oregano
1/4 teaspoon garlic
  powder

Heat oven to 350°. Wash and cut up chicken. Place in an 11-
by 9- by 2-inch pan. Peel potatoes and slice into one-half
inch thick pieces. Mix all ingredients with potatoes and pour
over chicken. Bake in oven for one hour until chicken and
potatoes are tender.

Serves: six to eight.

ENCHILADAS SUIZAS

1 whole chicken breast
water
1/4 small onion
1 bay leaf
4 peppercorns
salt and pepper
1 pound fresh tomatillos or
  1 cup drained canned
  tomatillos
1/2 small onion
1 large garlic clove

1 tablespoon packed fresh
  cilantro leaves
1 serrano chile or other small
  hot chile, seeded
2 tablespoons vegetable oil
6 corn tortillas
6 ounces Monterey Jack
  cheese, coarsely shredded
  (1 to 1 1/2 cups)
2 cups sour cream

Place chicken breast in a large saucepan with water to cover.
Add one-quarter onion, bay leaf, peppercorns and salt to
taste. Bring to a boil; reduce heat. Cover and simmer 45
minutes. Cool chicken breast in broth. Drain, reserving one
cup broth. Remove meat from bones and shred chicken.

Add salt and pepper to taste. If using fresh tomatillos, remove husks. Wash tomatillos and place in medium saucepan. Add one-half inch water. Bring to a boil then reduce
heat. Cover and simmer 10 minutes or until tender; drain.
Cool slightly. Do not cook canned tomatillos. Place cooked or
canned tomatillos in blender or food processor with one-half
onion, garlic, cilantro and chile. Process until pureed. Heat
two tablespoons oil in a medium saucepan. Add pureed
tomatillo mixture. Cook two to three minutes. Add reserved
chicken broth and one-half teaspoon salt. Bring to a boil;
reduce heat. Cover and simmer sauce 15 minutes. Add one
cup sour cream. Preheat oven to 350°. Heat one-quarter cup
oil in a medium skillet. With tongs, carefully place one
tortilla at a time in hot oil. Hold in oil three to five seconds
until softened. Quickly turn tortilla and soften other side
three to five seconds. Drain over skillet or on paper towels.
Place a spoonful of the shredded chicken on tortilla. Roll up
and place seam-side down in a shallow baking dish. When
all enchiladas are assembled, cover with sauce and top with
cheese. Bake 15 to 20 minutes, until cheese is melted and
bubbling. To serve, top with sour cream.

Serves: three.

*"For the first sixteen years of my life, I ate every Sunday supper
with my grandparents. Although my grandmother was from
Sicily, she prepared each week without fail the same meal: broiled
chicken, red wine with peaches, salad, bread and Entemann's cake.
Needless to say, I have never cooked broiled chicken and I never
cook the same menu twice!"*

SOFT CHICKEN BREAST

3 whole boneless, skinless
  chicken breasts
1/2 cup flour
1 teaspoon salt
1/4 teaspoon nutmeg
1/4 teaspoon black pepper

6 tablespoons butter
1 1/2 cups heavy cream
1/4 cup wine
1/2 pound mushrooms,
  sliced

Heat oven to 300°. Place chicken between waxed paper and
pound. Mix flour, salt, nutmeg and pepper. Coat chicken
with flour mixture. Brown chicken in butter, simmer for two
minutes and remove from stove. Remove chicken from the
pan and reserve the juices. Mix the cream and wine with the
reserved juices. Cover and simmer five minutes. Add
chicken back into cream sauce. Cook mushrooms in a separate pan. Pour chicken and sauce into a casserole baking
dish. Top with mushrooms. Bake for 20 minutes.

Serves: four.

CREAM CHEESE CHICKEN BREASTS

2 boneless, skinless chicken
  breasts halves
paprika
pepper
2 tablespoons butter or
  margarine, melted
2 tablespoons brandy
1/4 cup water
1/4 teaspoon dry mustard
1/4 teaspoon dried whole
  basil

1/4 teaspoon celery seeds
1/4 teaspoon ground ginger
1/4 teaspoon dried parsley
  flakes
1/4 teaspoon garlic powder
1 3-ounce package cream
  cheese, cubed
1 tablespoon slivered almonds,
  toasted

Sprinkle chicken breasts lightly with paprika and pepper.
Cook chicken in butter in a heavy skillet 12 minutes or until
done, turning once. Remove chicken and keep warm. Add
brandy to drippings in skillet; cook on high heat, stirring

constantly, until liquid is reduced to one tablespoon. Add water, mustard, basil, celery seeds, ginger, parsley, garlic powder and cream cheese. Cook over low heat, stirring constantly with a wire whisk until mixture is smooth. Pour sauce over chicken breasts. Sprinkle with almonds.

Serves: two.

CHICKEN MACADAMIA

6 whole, boneless, skinless chicken breasts	2 tablespoons brandy
peanut oil	2 tablespoons soy sauce
Batter	salt to taste
2 eggs	Sweet Sour Sauce
1/2 cup flour	4 tablespoons brown sugar
1/4 cup cornstarch	2 tablespoons soy sauce
1/2 cup cold water	2 tablespoons cornstarch
1 inch ginger root, minced	1/4 cup vinegar
1 medium onion, grated	1/4 cup cold water
1/2 teaspoon black pepper	macadamia nuts for garnish
2 tablespoons peanut oil	fried rice

Cut each chicken breast into six pieces. Mix batter ingredients thoroughly in a blender. Marinate chicken in batter for at least 20 minutes. Fry in peanut oil in a deep fryer at 350° for eight to 10 minutes or until done. Mix ingredients for sweet and sour sauce and simmer over low heat for 15 minutes. Serve cooked chicken on a bed of fried rice with sweet and sour sauce and a garnish of shaved and whole macadamia nuts.

Serves: 8 to 10.

CHICKEN BUNDLES WITH BACON BOWS

12 whole, boneless, skinless chicken breasts
1 cup molasses
1/2 teaspoon ground ginger
1/4 teaspoon garlic powder
2 tablespoons Worcestershire sauce
1/4 cup soy sauce
1/4 cup olive oil
1/4 cup lemon juice
2 pounds fresh mushrooms, slices and divided
20 green onions, sliced and divided
1/2 cup butter, melted and divided
1 teaspoon spike seasoning, divided
24 slices bacon, uncooked
Fresh dill sprigs for garnish

Place each chicken breast between two sheets of waxed paper or heavy duty plastic wrap. Flatten to one-quarter inch thickness using a meat mallet or rolling pin. Place chicken in a large shallow dish, set aside. Combine molasses, ginger, garlic powder, Worcestershire sauce, soy sauce, olive oil, and lemon juice. Pour over chicken and marinate in refrigerator eight hours or more. Cook half each of mushrooms and green onion in one-quarter cup butter in a large skillet over medium-high heat, stirring constantly, until liquid evaporates. Stir in one-half teaspoon spike seasoning. Set vegetables aside. Repeat process. Remove chicken from marinade, reserving marinade. For each chicken bundle, lay two slices bacon to form an X; place breast in center of bacon. Top with three tablespoons mushroom mixture. Fold over sides and ends of chicken to make a square. Secure with wooden picks. Pull bacon around and secure with wooden picks. Grill chicken, covered, over low coals, about 300°, 45 to 50 minutes or until done, turning and basting with remaining marinade every 15 minutes. Remove wooden picks before serving.

Spike seasoning, a blend of 39 herbs, spices and flavorings, can be found in the spice section at many supermarkets.

Serves: 12.

SOUTHWEST CHICKEN CHEESE AND PASTA

3-4 boneless, skinless chicken breasts
2 cloves garlic, minced
juice of 2 limes
1/2 teaspoon dried oregano
4 cups tender, cooked spaghetti, (8 ounces dried)
2 cups spicy tomato juice or regular tomato juice with splashes of Worcestershire sauce
2 chopped pickled hot peppers (without seeds)
1 red onion, halved and sliced
4 tablespoons chopped fresh cilantro
salt and pepper, to taste
1 cup shredded iceberg lettuce
1/2 cup shredded Cheddar cheese

Cut chicken into bite sized chunks and put in a zip lock bag with garlic, lime juice and oregano. Marinate 20 minutes at room temperature. Cook spaghetti until tender according to package directions. Meanwhile, brown chicken quickly with its marinade in a nonstick skillet sprayed with cooking spray. Remove chicken and its marinade juices; set aside. In the same skillet, combine tomato juice, hot peppers, onion, cilantro and seasonings. Simmer uncovered five to eight minutes until thickened. Add browned chicken to pan and heat through. To serve, drain pasta and arrange on platter. Pour over tomato-onion mixture. Surround with lettuce and top with cheese.

Serves: four.

$\mathcal{F}$ONTINA BAKED CHICKEN

1/2 cup flour
1/4 teaspoon dried oregano
1/4 teaspoon pepper
1/4 teaspoon paprika
1/8 teaspoon red pepper
1/4 teaspoon poultry
   seasoning
2 tablespoons Parmesan
   cheese
6 boneless, skinless chicken
   breast halves

2 eggs, beaten
1/2 cup butter or margarine,
   divided
1/2 pound mushrooms,
   halved
1/2 pound diced cooked
   ham
2 cups (8 ounces) shredded
   Fontina cheese, divided

Combine flour, oregano, pepper, paprika, red pepper, poultry seasoning and Parmesan cheese. Mix well. Dip chicken breasts in beaten eggs and dredge in flour mixture. Melt one-quarter cup butter in large skillet. Add chicken and cook 10 minutes on each side or until golden brown. Remove chicken and drain on paper towels. Place in cooking dish. Heat oven to 350°. Add remaining butter to skillet. Sauté mushroom four minutes or until tender, drain. Lay mushrooms and ham over chicken breasts. Sprinkle with one cup Fontina cheese. Cover and bake in oven for 35 minutes. Uncover and sprinkle with remaining cheese. Bake for five more minutes.

Serves: six.

$\mathcal{L}$EMON-BASTED PHEASANTS

2 pheasants
2 lemons
1 cup white wine

1 cup pineapple juice
2 tablespoons soy sauce
1 tablespoon lemon pepper

Wash and clean hens. Pierce the lemons in several places and place a lemon inside each hen. Mix together wine, pineapple juice, soy sauce, and lemon pepper. Baste hens with marinade. Place in roasting pan. Bake hens at 350° for one hour and 15 minutes, basting in marinade as it bakes.

Serves: two.

CORNBREAD-STUFFED CORNISH GAME HENS

1 6-ounce package cornbread stuffing mix
3/4 cup water
1/2 cup sliced celery
1 8-ounce container cream cheese with chives and onions, divided
1/2 cup fresh cranberries, sliced in half
1/4 cup coarsely chopped walnuts
4 1- to 1 1/2-pound Cornish game hens
vegetable oil
parsley sprigs, cranberries for garnish

Mix seasoning pack from stuffing mix with water and celery in a saucepan; bring to a boil. Cover, reduce heat and simmer for five minutes. Add stuffing mix, one-quarter cup cream cheese, cranberries, and walnuts. Cover; remove from heat. Let stand five minutes. Remove giblets from hens. Rinse hens with cold water and pat dry. Gently loosen skin on breast of each hen. Spread remaining cream cheese evenly under skin; replace skin. Stuff hens with cranberry mixture and tie the legs together with a string. Place hens, breast side up in a shallow roasting pan and brush with oil. Bake at 325° for one to one and one-half hours or until juices run clear when thigh of hen is pierced. Garnish.

Serves: four.

Cooling off at Rural Hall (San Jose Area).

$\mathscr{S}$IRLOIN WITH GREEN PEPPERCORN SAUCE

1 1/2 tablespoons drained
  green peppercorns
1 1/2 tablespoons country
  style Dijon mustard
1 tablespoon butter, room
  temperature

2 teaspoons flour
1 1/2 tablespoons olive oil
1 16-ounce sirloin steak,
  1 1/2 inches thick
3/4 cup beef broth
1/2 cup whipping cream

Mash peppercorns in small shallow bowl. Add mustard, butter and flour. Mix well. Heat oil in heavy large skillet over high heat. Season steak with salt and pepper and cook to desired doneness, about five minutes per side for medium-rare. Transfer steak to plate and tent with foil. Pour off drippings from skillet. Add broth and cream to same skillet and boil until sauce thickens slightly, about three minutes. Add peppercorn mixture, boil until sauce thickens enough to coat spoon whisking constantly, about one minute. Season with salt and pepper. Arrange steaks on plate and spoon sauce over steaks.

Serves: two.

A Thanksgiving Hunt, Deerwood Area.

BEEF STEW WITH BREW

4 pounds top or bottom round
  of beef
1/2 cup whole wheat flour
1/3 cup olive oil
2 1/2 pounds yellow onions,
  coarsely chopped
3 large garlic cloves, peeled
  and chopped
1 6-ounce can tomato paste
1 13 3/4-ounce can beef broth
1 cup ale or beer

2 bay leaves
1 teaspoon dried basil
  leaves
1/2 teaspoon salt
1 teaspoon dry thyme
1 10-ounce package frozen
  peas
1 12-ounce bag baby
  carrots or 1 10-ounce
  package frozen baby
  carrots

Cut beef into one and one-half inch cubes, trimming fat as
you go. On a sheet of waxed paper, toss beef in flour until
evenly coated. In a large heavy sauce pot, over medium
high heat, heat two tablespoons oil until very hot. Add a few
pieces of meat and cook until well browned on all sides.
Remove browned pieces with a slotted spoon and set aside.
Continue with remaining beef, adding more oil to the sauce
pot as necessary. Brown the meat well; if you don't, the
flavor will be weak and the color pale. Add the onions and
garlic to the sauce pot and cook, stirring frequently, until
soft, but not browned. Stir in the tomato paste and cook,
stirring, one minute. Add beef broth, ale or beer, bay leaves,
thyme leaves and salt. Return the beef to the pot. Heat to
boiling, over high heat. Reduce heat to low, partially cover
and simmer stew slowly for about one and one-half hours or
until meat is tender when pierced by a fork.* Add peas and
carrots and cook 10 minutes more or until vegetables are
tender-crisp.

*Stew can be made ahead up to this point; cool and refrigerate up
to two days. Before serving, heat to boiling, add vegetables and
proceed with the remaining steps.*

Serves: eight.

MEATBALLS IN CHIPOTLE SAUCE

<u>Meatballs</u>
1 pound very lean ground beef
1 pound ground turkey
2 eggs or 4 ounces egg substitute
1/2 cup dry bread crumbs
1/2 cup milk (skim)
2 tablespoons finely chopped onion
2 tablespoons snipped fresh cilantro
2 teaspoons salt
1/2 teaspoon pepper
4 cloves minced garlic

<u>Chipotle Sauce</u>
2 to 4 dried chipotle chiles
1 small finely chopped onion (about 1/4 cup)
2 cloves garlic, minced
4 medium tomatoes, finely chopped (about 3 cups)
1 cup beef broth
1/4 cup finely chopped carrot
1/4 cup finely chopped celery
1/4 cup snipped fresh cilantro
1/2 teaspoon salt
1/4 teaspoon pepper
1/2 teaspoon cumin

Cover chiles for chipotle sauce with warm water. Let stand until softened, about one hour. Drain and finely chop or blend in blender or food processor until smooth. Cook and stir onion in two quart saucepan until transparent. Stir in chiles and remaining ingredients. Mix remaining ingredients; shape into one and one-half inch balls. Heat sauce and meatballs to boiling then reduce heat. Cover and simmer until meatballs are done, about 20 minutes. Serve with hot cooked noodles or low fat green rice. (page 84)

Serves: eight.

Rex and Sonny-Ready for the hunt, 1925.

$\mathcal{V}$EAU A LA WENDE

4 veal cutlets
2 tablespoons butter
2 green onions, sliced
1 clove garlic, pressed

juice of one lemon
1/4 cup Parmesan cheese
2 tablespoons sesame seeds
1 tablespoon Dijon mustard

Melt butter in skillet. Add onion and garlic. Add veal. Cook two to three minutes over medium heat. Sprinkle with Parmesan cheese, lemon juice and sesame seeds. Fifteen minutes later spread one side of cutlets with Dijon mustard. Turn occasionally. Cook 30-45 minutes at a simmering temperature.

Serves: two to four.

$\mathcal{T}$EQUILA TENDERLOIN

1/4 cup prepared mustard
2 pounds pork tenderloin
1/4 cup vegetable oil
2 cloves garlic, cut into
 halves
1/4 cup carrot, chopped
1/4 cup celery, chopped
1/4 cup lime juice
1/4 cup tequila
2 teaspoons ground red
 chiles
1 teaspoon cumin

1 teaspoon salt
1 teaspoon dried oregano
 leaves
1 teaspoon dried thyme leaves
1/4 teaspoon pepper
4 medium tomatoes, chopped
 (about 4 cups)
1 small onion, chopped (about
 1/4 cup)
1 bay leaf
1/4 cup snipped parsley

Spread mustard over pork tenderloin. Heat oil and garlic in 10-inch skillet until hot. Cook pork in oil over medium heat until brown. Remove garlic. Stir in remaining ingredients except parsley. Heat to boiling; reduce heat. Cover and simmer until pork is done, about 30 minutes. Remove bay leaf. Sprinkle with parsley.

Serves: six.

ROAST PORK WITH SPICED CHERRY SAUCE

1 3 to 4 pound boneless rolled
  pork loin roast
1 teaspoon salt
1 teaspoon pepper
1 teaspoon rubbed sage
1 16-ounce can pitted sour red
  cherries, undrained
1 1/2 cups sugar
1/4 cup white vinegar
12 whole cloves

1 3-inch stick cinnamon
1/4 cup cornstarch
1 tablespoon lemon juice
1 tablespoon melted butter
  or margarine
3 to 4 drops red food
  coloring
garnishes: purple and
  green kale, lemon
  wedges and rind strips

Heat oven to 325°. Sprinkle roast with salt, pepper and sage.
Place, fat side up on a rack in a shallow roasting pan. Insert
meat thermometer into thickest part of meat. Bake for one
and one-half to two hours or until meat thermometer registers 160°. Drain cherries; reserve liquid and add water to
make three-quarters cup, if necessary. Combine one-half cup
cherry liquid, sugar, vinegar, cloves and cinnamon in a
saucepan. Bring to a boil; reduce heat, and simmer, uncovered, 10 minutes. Remove and discard spices. Combine
cornstarch and remaining one-quarter cup cherry liquid; stir
into hot liquid. Cook over medium heat, stirring constantly,
one minute or until thickened and bubbly. Stir in cherries,
lemon juice, butter and food coloring. Place roast on a platter; garnish if desired. Serve with sauce.

Serves: six to eight.

DOUBLE-FRUIT GLAZED PORK CHOPS

6 rib pork chops, 6 to 8
  ounces each
salt and pepper to taste
1 cup brown sugar
1/4 cup pineapple juice
1/4 cup honey
1 teaspoon dry mustard
3 whole cloves
3 whole coriander seeds,
  crushed

6 slices orange
6 slices lemon
6 slices lime
6 maraschino cherries
1 1/2 tablespoons cornstarch
2 tablespoons water
1/2 teaspoon salt
1 lemon slice

Heat oven to 350°. Brown chops in skillet; season with salt and pepper and place in a shallow baking pan. Combine brown sugar, pineapple juice, honey, dry mustard, cloves and coriander. Spoon about one tablespoon for the sauce over each chop. Bake uncovered about one hour and 15 minutes, basting with half of the sauce. With wooden pick, skewer one slice of orange, lemon and lime on each chop; top with a cherry. Baste fruit with the remaining sauce and bake an additional 10 minutes. Measure pan juices; skim off fat and add enough water to make one and one-third cups. Blend cornstarch with two tablespoons water. Stir into juices. Add one-quarter teaspoon salt and lemon slice. Cook, stirring constantly until sauce is thickened and bubbly. Simmer two or three minutes, stirring occasionally. Remove lemon slice and serve sauce with chops.

Serves: six.

*B*AKED SAUSAGE FETTUCCINE

1 pound fettucine, cooked and well drained
2 tablespoons butter
1 pound hot Italian sausage
1 tablespoon olive oil
1 medium-sized onion, finely chopped
1 large banana pepper, finely chopped
1/2 cup sliced pitted ripe olives
1/4 cup finely chopped mix of fresh parsley and basil

1/2 teaspoon freshly ground black pepper
4 eggs, beaten
4 thinly sliced tomatoes
2 cups grated Gruyére cheese
2 cups grated mozzarella cheese
4 tablespoons grated Parmesan cheese

Preheat oven to 375°. Toss hot fettuccine with butter in mixing bowl and cover. Remove sausage casings and finely chop meat. Brown sausage in heated olive oil; pour off fat. Add onion and banana pepper; cook five minutes. Combine sausage mixture, olives, parsley-basil mix, pepper and noodles. Stir in eggs and toss to combine well. Lightly butter and flour a springform pan. Press one-third of the pasta mixture on bottom; layer one-third of the tomatoes over pasta. Sprinkle the Gruyere and mozzarella cheese over the tomatoes. Repeat the layers two more times. Sprinkle the Parmesan cheese over the top. Cover with foil and bake 50 minutes until set. To serve, slice in wedges.

Serves: six to eight.

$\mathscr{R}$OAST DUCK WITH KUMQUAT SAUCE

1 4 to 5 pound domestic duckling

Kumquat Sauce (recipe follows)

Kumquat Sauce
3 preserved kumquats
1/2 cup water
1/3 cup orange juice
1 tablespoon cornstarch

1 teaspoon instant chicken bouillon
2 tablespoons toasted, chopped pecans
1 tablespoon orange liqueur

Heat oven to 375°. Rinse duck and pat dry. Tuck drumsticks under the band of skin across the tail. Skewer neck skin to back. Twist wing tips under back. Prick skin well all over. Place bird, breast side up, on rack in a shallow roasting pan. Insert meat thermometer into thigh meat. Roast, uncovered, for one and three-quarter to two and one-quarter hours or until meat thermometer registers 180° to 185°. Remove fat during roasting. Cover and let stand 15 minutes. For sauce, thinly slice preserved kumquats removing seeds. In a small saucepan, combine water, orange juice, cornstarch and in-stant chicken bouillon granules. Cook and stir until bubbly. Cook and stir two minutes more. Add kumquats, toasted chopped pecans and orange liqueur; heat through. If desired, garnish duck with lemon leaves and additional kumquats. Serve with kumquat sauce.

Serves: six.

$\mathcal{G}$ORGONZOLA BUTTER GRILLED LAMB CHOPS

1/2 cup olive oil
1/4 cup chopped shallots
4 teaspoons minced fresh
  rosemary or 2 teaspoons
  dried
2 tablespoons minced garlic
4 7 to 8-ounce lamb chops

Gorgonzola Butter
1/2 cup plus 1 teaspoon
  unsalted butter, room
  temperature
2 teaspoons minced shallots
2 teaspoons minced garlic
4 ounces Gorgonzola cheese
1 tablespoon olive oil
1 tablespoon fresh lemon juice

Whisk olive oil, shallots and rosemary in small bowl. Season with salt and pepper. Place chops in baking dish. Pour marinade over and turn to coat. Marinate overnight or at least three hours. Melt one teaspoon in heavy skillet over medium heat. Add shallots and garlic. Sauté one minute. Set aside. Use electric mixer and beat remaining one-half cup butter and cheese in bowl until fluffy. Add shallot mixture, oil and lemon juice and beat to blend. Season. Drop mixture onto plastic wrap and form a log. Roll log and chill three hours or up to a week ahead. Grill lamb chops to desired doneness (six minutes per side for medium rare). Transfer chops to plate. Unwrap Gorgonzola butter and cut into one-half inch wide slices. Place one butter slice on chop and serve immediately.

Serves: four.

Preceding Page: Soup from Tailgate at the TPC
For Menu: See Page 237

The tournament Players Championship annually plays host to the best golfers in the PGA. While being televised nationally, it is a favorite spectator event among the locals.

When Henry Flagler built the Continental Club Hotel at Atlantic Beach in 1901, it sported a nine-hole golf course. The hotel was later destroyed by fire.

Photograph is from collections at The Jacksonville Historical Society Archives.

MAGNIFICENT MINESTRONE

1 cup navy beans, dried
2 14 1/2-ounce cans chicken
   broth
2 teaspoons salt
1 small head cabbage, cored
   and shredded
4 carrots, peeled and sliced
2 medium potatoes, peeled
   and diced
1 28-ounce can Italian plum
   tomatoes, chopped
2 medium onions, chopped
1 stalk celery, chopped
1 large fresh tomato, peeled
   and chopped
1 clove garlic, minced
1/4 cup olive oil

1/4 cup parsley, chopped
1/4 teaspoon pepper
1 cup vermicelli, broken
   into pieces
Pesto Sauce
1/4 cup butter, softened
   (no substitute)
1/4 cup grated Parmesan
   cheese
1/2 cup chopped parsley
1 clove garlic, minced
1 teaspoon basil
1/2 teaspoon marjoram
1/4 cup olive oil
1/4 cup chopped walnuts
   or pine nuts

Cover beans with water and soak overnight. Drain. Measure chicken broth and add water to measure three quarts. Add salt. Cook beans in broth mixture until almost tender. Add cabbage, carrots, potatoes and canned tomatoes. Sauté onions, celery, fresh tomato and garlic in olive oil then add to soup. Stir in parsley and pepper. Add vermicelli to soup 15 minutes before serving. Serve hot in bowls with a spoonful of pesto sauce in each bowl.

DO NOT OMIT pesto sauce as it contains ALL the seasonings!

Serves: 10-12.

"My mother-in-law's gumbo is fabulous! There was a time, however, when I had had too much of it! I found myself a new bride in Atlanta, living in an apartment, and I couldn't even boil water. My mother-in-law, fearing her son would starve, sent a dozen frozen containers of her famous gumbo. For two solid weeks, we ate nothing but gumbo. After that I found a cookbook and decided to learn how to cook!"

ZUCCHINI SOUP

2 medium onions, sliced
4 zucchini, unpeeled and
 sliced in 1/4 inch pieces
 (about 3 cups)
4 tablespoons olive oil
6 cups chicken stock or low
 salt broth

1 10-ounce package frozen
 lima beans
1 cup frozen peas
1 teaspoon curry
salt and pepper to taste

Saute´ onions and zucchini in oil for 10 minutes in heavy, medium sized saucepan. Add chicken stock and bring to a boil. Add lima beans and peas. When mixture boils reduce heat and simmer 20 minutes. Place in blender and blend. Add curry, salt and pepper to taste, then serve.

Serves: six.

BAKED POTATO SOUP

4 large baking potatoes
2/3 cup butter
2/3 cup flour
6 cups milk
3/4 teaspoon salt
1/2 teaspoon pepper

4 green onions, chopped
 and divided
1 jar bacon bits, divided
1 1/4 cups shredded
 cheddar cheese, divided
1 8-ounce carton sour cream

Wash potatoes and prick with fork. Bake at 400° for one hour. Let cool. Scoop out potatoes and discard skins. Melt butter in heavy sauce pan on low heat. Add flour and stir until smooth. Cook one minute stirring constantly. Gradually add milk. Cover until thick and add potato pulp, salt, pepper, two tablespoons green onion, one-half cup bacon bits and one cup cheese. Cook until totally heated. Stir in sour cream adding extra cream for desired thickness. Serve with remaining onion, bacon and cheese.

Serves: 8 to 12.

*S*HRIMP GUMBO

1/2 cup oil
3 cloves garlic
2 large onions
3 pounds peeled raw
  shrimp
1/2 cup flour

2 tablespoons filé powder
2 quarts water
1 8-ounce can tomato sauce
1 16-ounce tomatoes with
  chiles

Heat oil in large heavy pot, or iron skillet. Sauté garlic and onions. Coat raw shrimp in flour mixed with filé powder. Heat water to a boil in large two quart pan. Cook shrimp for two minutes. Reduce heat and add tomato sauce and can of tomatoes with chiles. Enjoy.

Yield: three quarts.

*M*ULLIGATAWNY SOUP

1/4 cup finely chopped
  onion
1 1/2 teaspoons curry
  powder
2 tablespoons oil
1 tart apple, peeled, cored
  and chopped
1/4 cup chopped carrot
1/4 cup chopped celery
2 tablespoons chopped red
  bell pepper

3 tablespoons flour
4 cups chicken broth
1 16-ounce can tomatoes,
  chopped with juices
1 tablespoon chopped parsley
2 teaspoon lemon juice
1 teaspoon sugar
2 whole cloves
1/4 teaspoon salt
dash of pepper
1 cup diced cooked chicken

Cook onion and curry powder in oil in large saucepan until onion is tender. Stir in apple, carrot, celery and red pepper. Cook, stirring occasionally, until vegetables are crisp-tender, about five minutes. Sprinkle flour over vegetables. Stir to mix well. Add broth, tomatoes, parsley, lemon juice, sugar, cloves, salt and pepper. Bring to a boil, then add chicken. Simmer for 30 minutes, stirring occasionally.

Serves: six.

ℬRUNSWICK SOUP STEW

1 3 to 3 1/2 pound broiler
   fryer
1 pound boneless beef, cut
   into 1 inch cubes
1 pound boneless pork
1 gallon water
6 medium potatoes, peeled
   and cubed
1 large onion, chopped

1 cup frozen whole kernel
   corn
1 cup frozen lima beans
1/2 cup finely chopped
   celery
1 hot red pepper, whole
2 tablespoons salt
18 ounces bar-b-que sauce

Combine chicken, beef, pork, water, potatoes and onion in a
large Dutch oven; bring to a boil. Cover, reduce heat and
simmer two hours or until meat is tender. Remove meat
from broth. Save broth and cool meat completely. Skin, bone
and chop chicken. Coarsely chop meat; set aside. Skim off
and discard surface of broth. Measure broth, and return
three quarts to Dutch oven. Add chopped meats and remaining
ingredients. Bring mixture to a boil. Reduce heat and
simmer two hours, stirring often. Add additional reserved
broth and water, if needed. Discard red pepper pod.

Yield: five quarts.

ℋARVEST SOUP IN A PUMPKIN

1 well shaped, medium
   sized ripe pumpkin (approximately 4-6 pounds)
black pepper
1/4 cup brown sugar
1/2 pound Gruyere cheese,
   grated
1/2 pound baby Swiss
   cheese, grated
1/4 pound sharp Cheddar
   cheese, grated

3 cups heavy cream
1 teaspoon allspice
1 teaspoon nutmeg
2 teaspoons basil
2 teaspoons parsley
6 green onions, chopped
2 1/2 cups seasoned croutons
1 cup cooked ham, chopped

Preheat oven at 350°. Cut lid from pumpkin and reserve. Scrape inside of pumpkin clean, leaving a good strong bottom; sprinkle with black pepper. By hand, rub brown sugar to coat inside of pumpkin. In large saucepan over medium-low heat, combine cheeses, cream, seasonings and onions. Heat until melted and blended together. Put two layers of croutons and ham inside pumpkin. Pour cheese mixture over croutons and ham. Cover pumpkin with foil and bake in preheated oven 50 minutes. Stir occasionally. Remove pumpkin from oven and place on serving platter. Top with the pumpkin lid.

Serves: six.

BEEF SOUP WITH MEATBALLS

3 small fresh hot green peppers
1 pound lean ground beef
2 cloves garlic, crushed
1 teaspoon salt
1/4 cup tomato sauce
1 teaspoon chili powder
1 teaspoon ground cumin
1 tablespoon parsley, chopped
1/2 cup bread crumbs
2 eggs, beaten
3 tablespoons butter
6 cups hot basic brown soup stock
1/2 dry red wine

Remove seeds from peppers and chop. Mix with beef, garlic, salt, tomato sauce, chili powder, cumin, parsley, bread crumbs and egg. Blend. Form the meat mixture into 43 meatballs, and brown them in butter. Add meatballs to soup stock with wine. Simmer 10 minutes. Add salt to taste.

This blend of herbs and spices, coupled with the rich beef stock and the small meatballs, offer a very unusual full-meal soup.

Serves: 12 to 15.

CREAMED VEGETABLE SOUP

2 cups chicken or beef broth
1 cup broccoli or spinach, chopped very fine
1 small onion, chopped very fine
1/4 cup parsley, chopped fine

salt
pepper
pinch of thyme
sherry wine, to taste
1 cup light cream
2 egg yolks

Simmer the finely chopped vegetables in broth. Stir in onion and parsley while cooking. Add seasoning to taste. When vegetables are tender (takes only a few minutes), put mixture and cream in top of double boiler over hot but not boiling water. In a small bowl, beat yolks until thoroughly blended. Slowly add this mixture to soup and stir with wooden spoon until thickened. It is done when soup coats the spoon with a slight film. Do not overcook or let soup boil as it will curdle.

Serves: six.

SCOTCH BROTH SOUP

2 1/2 cups diced lamb
3 leeks, sliced thin
1/4 cup butter
4 chicken bouillon cubes
salt and pepper

1/2 cup pearl barley
1 cup diced carrots
1 cup chopped celery
1/2 cup chopped parsley

Sauté lamb and leeks in butter for 10 minutes. Stir often. Add 3 quarts water, bouillon cubes, salt and pepper. Bring to boil, cover and simmer one hour. Add barley, simmer for another hour. Add carrots, celery and parsley then simmer uncovered 15 minutes.

Serves: six.

CHILI BLANCO

2 cups dried Great Northern
white beans
3 whole chicken breasts,
skinned
3 1/2 cups water
2 tablespoons olive oil
2 cups finely chopped onion
4 garlic cloves, minced
2 4-ounce cans chopped
green chilies
1 serrano or jalapeno chili,
cored, seeded and minced
2 teaspoons ground cumin

1 tablespoon minced fresh
oregano, or 1 1/2 teaspoons
dried oregano
1/4 teaspoon ground cloves
1/4 teaspoon cayenne pepper
3 cups chicken stock
salt to taste
2 cups grated Monterey Jack
cheese
garnish with diced tomatoes,
additional grated cheese,
chopped green onions,
chopped fresh cilantro

Place beans in a heavy, large pot and cover with plenty of water. Soak for one hour. Put chicken breasts in a large skillet; cover with three and one-half cups water. Bring to boil and simmer, covered, 30 minutes. Remove from pan, reserving liquid and let cool. When chicken is cool, remove bones and shred the meat. Drain beans, rinse and set aside. In same pot heat oil over medium heat. Add onions and cook, stirring for 10 minutes. Add garlic, chilies, cumin, oregano, cloves and cayenne pepper and cook two minutes more. Add beans, stock and reserved chicken cooking liquid. Bring to a boil, cover and simmer, stirring occasionally until beans are tender, about two hours. Add salt to taste and adjust seasoning. Before serving, add shredded chicken and cheese. Stir until cheese is melted and chicken is heated through. Garnish, if desired, with diced tomatoes, grated cheese, chopped green onions and chopped cilantro.

Serves: six to eight.

$\mathscr{F}$IRESIDE CHILI

2 pounds chili meat
1 pound ground beef
2 tablespoons bacon drippings
1 pint hot water
1 10 1/2-ounce can tomato puree
1 tablespoon hot pepper sauce
1 chili pepper pod or more, to taste

2 large onions, finely chopped
2 cloves garlic, finely chopped
3 heaping tablespoons chili powder
1 tablespoon oregano
1 tablespoon cumin
1 teaspoon paprika
1 teaspoon ground mustard
1/4 teaspoon cayenne pepper
1 tablespoon salt

Brown meats. Add bacon drippings and cook five minutes. Add hot water, tomato puree, hot pepper sauce, pepper pod, onion and garlic. Simmer 30 minutes. Pour in remainder of the ingredients and simmer slowly for one to two hours. Serve with crackers, raw onion, grated sharp Cheddar cheese and plenty of ice cold beer.

Serves: six to eight.

$\mathscr{C}$REAM OF SQUASH SOUP

1/4 cup margarine, melted
2 1/2 tablespoons oil
1 large onion, minced
2 cloves garlic, minced
3 pounds yellow squash, thinly sliced

4 cups chicken broth
1 cup light cream
3/4 teaspoon salt
1/2 teaspoon white pepper

Combine margarine and oil in a large Dutch oven. Add onion and garlic, sauté until tender. Stir in squash and chicken broth. Cover and simmer 15-20 minutes until squash is tender. Spoon one-third of mixture into blender and puree until smooth. Repeat with remaining squash mixture. Return all of pureed mixture to Dutch oven and stir in light cream, salt and pepper. Cook over low heat, stirring constantly until well heated. May be served hot or cold.

Serves: 8 to 10.

CURRIED CREAM OF BROCCOLI
With Rice and Lentils

1 large bunch broccoli, including stems, chopped
1 medium onion, chopped
6 cups chicken stock or 1/2
   cup Vogue (see note below)
   added to 6 cups water
2-3 teaspoons curry powder

1/2 cup brown rice
1/2 cup red lentils
1 1/2 cups water
1 cup cream or milk
salt and pepper

Place broccoli and onion in pot with stock and curry. Simmer until tender. Wash rice and lentils and cook together with one and one-half cups of water until rice is tender but chewy. Place small portions of broccoli and stock in a blender or food processor and puree. Place creamed soup in a different pot and add milk, rice, beans, salt and pepper to taste.

Vogue broth is a chemical-free and preservative-free powdered broth that can be found in health food stores.

Serves: 10.

After all the grandchildren were born, Christmas dinner became more complicated trying to accommodate all the in-laws. My mother decided to make dinner light and easy with my father's famous vegetable soup as the main entree. We were all anxiously awaiting for Christmas day to arrive so that we could dig into that big pot of soup my dad had been savoring for days. When dinner time arrived, my mother said she would warm the soup and soon a smell filled the house and it wasn't a good one. We checked the soup and the bottom was scorched. We tried to eat it off the top, but you could taste the scorched flavor that had made its way through the whole pot. We laughed and made the best of it and since then we do not let Mom near the soup.

CREAM OF CARROT SOUP

Stock
2 1/2 cups water
2 chicken-flavored broth
  packets or cubes
1 beef-flavored broth packet
  or cube
1 tablespoon chopped
  parsley
5 large carrots, thinly sliced,
  about 4 cups
5 stalks celery, thinly sliced,
  about 2 1/4 cups
1 small potato, chopped
1 small onion, chopped
1/4 teaspoon pepper
1/4 teaspoon salt or to taste

Seasoning
3 tablespoons butter
1 1/2 tablespoons cornstarch
1/4 teaspoon marjoram
1/4 teaspoon thyme, crumbled
1/4 teaspoon basil
1/2 teaspoon Angostura
2 cups milk
1 1/2 cups commercial sour
  cream, divided

Garnish
sour cream
chopped chives

Cook stock ingredients until very soft, about 30 to 40 minutes.
Puree in blender or mash through a sieve. Add the seasoning
and mix in blender. Pour mixture back into pan. Add milk,
mix well, and heat over low heat, stirring often, until it thickens, about five minutes. Add one cup sour cream; mix well.
Serve hot with garnish of sour cream and chopped chives.

Serves: six.

CHILLED RASPBERRY SOUP

1 1/2 tablespoons unflavored
  gelatin
1/3 cup cold water
3/4 cup hot water
3 10-ounce packages frozen
  raspberries, thawed
3 1/2 cups sour cream (28
  ounces)

1 1/3 cups pineapple juice
1 1/3 cups half and half
1 1/3 cups dry sherry
1/3 cup grenadine
2 tablespoons lemon juice
garnish: mint, whole
  raspberries

Soak gelatin in cold water for five minutes. Stir in hot water and dissolve over low heat. Push raspberries through a strainer to remove seeds, then puree. Combine with remaining ingredients and place in a glass bowl. Cover and refrigerate overnight. Garnish with mint and/or whole raspberries.

Great served as a first course for a luncheon. Leftover soup can be frozen for a yogurt-like snack.

Serves: 12.

KIELBASA STEW

4 tablespoons olive oil
2 pounds Polish Kielbasa
2 large onions
1 teaspoon salt
1 teaspoon garlic powder
1/2 teaspoon pepper
10 cups water (may substitute with clamato or tomato juice)

2 medium bay leaves
1 1/2 cups diced celery
1 1/2 cups sliced carrots
4 cups of diced potatoes
1 28-ounce can whole tomatoes (quartered) with juice
medium head of cabbage cut into chunks

Brown Kielbasa with onions in oil together with salt, garlic powder and pepper. Add water, bay leaves, celery and carrots and bring to a boil. When vegetables begin to soften, add potatoes and tomatoes. Boil until potatoes are almost done, then add cabbage and continue to boil until cabbage is tender, approximately 10 minutes. Remove bay leaves. The stew is ready to eat, but is better if it simmers for 30 minutes to one hour. This stew is great when placed in the refrigerator and eaten a couple of days later.

Yield: 24 10-ounce servings.

WILLIAMSBURG TURKEY SOUP

1 turkey carcass
4 quarts water
1 cup butter or margarine
1 cup flour
3 onions, chopped
2 large carrots, diced

2 stalks celery, diced
1 cup long grain rice, uncooked
2 teaspoons salt
3/4 teaspoon pepper
2 cups half and half

Place turkey carcass and water in large Dutch oven, bring to a boil. Cover, reduce heat and simmer one hour. Remove carcass from broth and pick meat from bones. Set meat and broth aside. Measure broth, add water, if necessary, to measure three quarts. Heat butter in Dutch oven, add flour and cook over medium heat five minutes. Roux will be light color. Stir in chopped onion, carrots and celery into roux and cook over medium heat 10 minutes, stirring often. Add reserved three quarts broth, turkey, rice, salt and pepper. Bring to a boil. Cover, reduce heat and simmer 20 minutes until rice is tender. Add half and half and cook until soup is thoroughly heated.

Yield: four and one-half quarts.

WILD RICE SOUP

1 cup wild rice
1 small onion, finely chopped
1/2 cup butter
1/2 cup flour
4 cups beef broth

1/4 teaspoon salt
1/4 teaspoon pepper
1 cup heavy cream
1 cup dry white wine

Cook rice according to directions. Uncover when done. Set aside. Sauté onion in butter for three minutes until softened. Sprinkle with flour, stirring until flour is cooked, but not browned then slowly add broth. Heat until well blended. Add remaining ingredients. Heat gently.

Serves: 10 to 12.

TORTILLA SOUP

3 tablespoons corn oil
4 coarsely chopped corn
   tortillas
6 cloves garlic, finely
   chopped
1 tablespoon chopped fresh
   epazote or 1 tablespoon
   chopped fresh cilantro
1 cup fresh onion puree
2 cups fresh tomato puree
1 tablespoon cumin powder
2 teaspoons chili powder
2 bay leaves

4 tablespoons canned
   tomato puree
2 quarts chicken stock
salt, to taste
cayenne pepper, to taste
garnish: 1 cooked chicken
   breast, cut into strips
1 avocado, peeled, pitted
   and cubed
1 cup shredded cheddar
   cheese
3 corn tortillas, cut into thin
   strips and fried crisp

Heat oil in a large saucepan over medium heat. Sauté tortillas with garlic and epazote over medium heat until tortillas are soft. Add onions and fresh tomato puree and bring to a boil. Add cumin, chili powder, bay leaves, canned tomato puree and chicken stock. Bring to a boil again, then reduce heat to simmer. Add salt and cayenne to taste and cook, stirring frequently, for 30 minutes. Skim fat from surface, if necessary. Strain and pour into warm soup bowls. Garnish each bowl with an equal portion of chicken breast, avocado, shredded cheese and crisp tortilla strips. Serve immediately.

Soup may be made one day ahead and gently reheated before serving.

Serves: 8 to 10.

PORK AND SQUASH STEW

1 pound pork shoulder
3 tablespoons flour
1/2 teaspoon salt
1/4 teaspoon pepper
4 teaspoons vegetable oil,
 divided
3 cups coarsely chopped
 onion

2 1/4 cups sliced carrot
1/2 teaspoon dried
 rosemary, crushed
1 12-ounce can beer
2 cups 1/2-inch cubed
 peeled butternut squash
 (about 1 pound)
2 teaspoons chopped fresh
 parsley

Trim fat from pork. Cut pork into three-quarter inch cubes and set aside. Combine flour, salt and pepper in a large zip-top heavy-duty plastic bag. Add pork to bag, seal bag and shake to coat. Heat two teaspoons vegetable oil in a large nonstick skillet over medium-high heat, and add pork, browning on all sides. Remove pork from skillet, and set aside. Add onion and carrot, and sauté five minutes or until onion is tender. Return pork to skillet; add rosemary and beer and bring to a boil. Cover, reduce heat, and simmer 30 minutes. Add the squash; cover and simmer an additional 25 minutes or until squash is tender. Ladle into individual bowls, and sprinkle each serving with one-half teaspoon parsley.

The stew can be frozen in an airtight freezer container. Thaw in the refrigerator.

Serves: four to six.

DRAGON'S BREATH

1/2 ounce dried shiitake
   mushrooms
1 cup hot water
vegetable cooking spray
1/2 teaspoon chili oil
1 cup fresh bean sprouts
1/2 cup sliced green onions
1/2 teaspoon bottled
   minced fresh garlic
3 tablespoons white wine
   vinegar

1 tablespoon low-sodium
   soy sauce
1/8 teaspoon white pepper
2 10 1/2-ounce cans low-
   salt chicken broth
1/2 10.5-ounce package
   firm tofu, drained and
   cubed
2 tablespoons cornstarch
2 tablespoons water
1 egg white, lightly beaten

Place mushrooms in a bowl and add hot water. Microwave on high two minutes. Let stand 15 minutes. Drain mushrooms; discard stems. Coarsely chop mushroom caps; set aside. Coat a large saucepan with cooking spray; add oil, and place over medium-high heat until hot. Add bean sprouts, green onions and garlic. Sauté three minutes or until tender. Add chopped mushroom caps, vinegar, soy sauce, white pepper, chicken broth and tofu then bring to a boil. Reduce heat, and simmer three minutes. Combine cornstarch and two tablespoons water, stirring with a wire whisk until blended. Add to soup, stirring constantly. Cook one minute or until thickened, stirring constantly. Remove from heat; slowly drizzle egg white into soup, stirring constantly with handle of a wooden spoon.

Yield: four cups.

ENGLISH CLUB SANDWICH

4 English muffins
8 slices turkey breast
8 slices ham

8 slices tomato
8 broccoli spears, blanched

Split muffins and lightly toast. Layer turkey, ham, tomato and broccoli on toasted muffin halves. Top with Hollandaise sauce and serve.

<u>Blender Hollandaise</u>
5 egg yolks
2 tablespoons lemon juice

1/4 teaspoon salt
1/4 teaspoon pepper
1 cup butter, melted

Blend egg yolks, lemon juice, salt and pepper in blender. With blender on, pour in hot butter, Continue until thoroughly blended.

Yield: eight open-faced sandwiches.

MONTE CRISTO SANDWICH

1 slice turkey ham
1 slice Swiss cheese

1 slice turkey breast
2 slices frozen French toast

Layer turkey ham, cheese and turkey breast between French toast. Place on ungreased baking sheet and heat in a 400° oven for 15 minutes. Sprinkle with powdered sugar or serve with raspberry jam.

Yield: one sandwich.

BREAKFAST SANDWICHES

12 slices white bread without crust
12 slices ham
12 slices American cheese
2 cups milk
6 eggs
dry mustard to taste
hot pepper sauce to taste
butter (enough to spread
on 12 slices bread front
and back)

Preheat oven at 350°. Butter 12 slices bread. Layer six slices
with ham and cheese. Place in a 9 x 12 baking pan. Put other
six buttered slices on top of ham and cheese. Mix milk, eggs
and other ingredients in bowl. Pour over bread, cover. Let
stand overnight in refrigerator. Remove from refrigerator
and let stand at room temperature for 30 minutes. Bake at
350° for 45 minutes to one hour.

This recipe must be made one day before serving.

Serves: six.

HOT HAM SANDWICHES

1/2 cup softened butter or
margarine
1/4 cup prepared or Dijon
mustard
1/4 cup diced onion
1 tablespoon poppy seeds
16 hamburger buns
2 pounds thinly sliced deli
ham
2 8-ounce packages
shredded Swiss cheese

Combine butter, mustard, onion and poppy seeds. Spread
mixture on cut surfaces of hamburger buns. Divide ham into
16 portions and place on bottom of each bun. Sprinkle
evenly with cheese. Cover with top of bun. Wrap each sandwich in aluminum foil. Bake at 350° for 20 minutes or until
thoroughly heated. Unwrap sandwiches, and cut each into
halves; spear each with a decorative pick.

*Sandwiches may be frozen up to one month before baking. Thaw
sandwiches in refrigerator overnight. Bake as directed.*

Yield: 16 sandwiches.

$\mathscr{S}$HRIMPLY DELICIOUS CROISSANDWICHES

1 10-ounce package frozen
  spinach
1 4 1/4-ounce can shrimp
1/4 cup minced onion
1/3 cup mayonnaise
1-2 tablespoons Dijon mustard
1/3 cup Macadamia nuts
  chopped

1/4 teaspoon celery salt
1/4 teaspoon Cavenders'
  seasoning
1/2 teaspoon fresh dill,
  chopped
3 croissants
3 slices Swiss cheese

Heat oven to 350°. Cook spinach according to package directions. Drain. Combine shrimp, onion, mayonnaise, mustard,
nuts, celery salt, Cavenders´ seasoning and dill. Mix well to
make shrimp salad filling. Slice croissants in half lengthwise.
Place slice of cheese on top of shrimp mixture. Replace the tops
of croissants. Bake for five to 10 minutes.

Yield: three croissants.

$\mathscr{I}$TALIAN BEEF

2 tablespoons of shortening
1 beef roast, 7 pounds, or 2
  beef roasts, 3 1/2 pounds
  each
salt and pepper, to taste

4 cups water
5 green peppers, sliced and
  chopped
1 teaspoon garlic salt
10 sandwich buns

Heat shortening in large Dutch oven. Season roast with salt and
pepper. Brown in hot shortening. Add water and simmer for
one hour and 30 minutes. Remove roast and cool. Slice thinly.
Return meat to liquid and add green peppers and garlic salt.
Simmer four hours. Serve on sandwich buns.

Great to have on hand.

Yield: 10 sandwiches.

CUCUMBER AND HAM SANDWICHES

4 ounces of cream cheese,
  softened
2 tablespoons mayonnaise
8 slices bread

1 cucumber, thinly sliced
4 slices of ham, cut into
  sandwich shapes
fresh dill for garnish

Soften the cream cheese and mix with mayonnaise. Remove the crust from the slices of bread and cut the bread into square, circles and triangle shapes. Spread cream cheese mixture on bread and place thinly sliced cucumber and ham slices on the bread. Place the ham on the bread first, then top with the cucumber. Garnish with fresh dill.

Foolishly simple, but oh, so good! Always a hit for tailgate and card parties.

Serves: 8 to 10.

FLORIDIAN PEANUT BUTTER SANDWICH

1/2 cup peanut butter
4 ounces Neufchatel cheese,
  softened
4 tablespoons orange juice
  concentrate

2 tablespoons finely grated
  carrots
1 tablespoon diced raisins,
  dates or currants
4 slices whole grain bread

Mix the peanut butter, orange juice, carrots, cream cheese and raisins. Spread on the bread.

Serves: four.

$\mathcal{B}$ACON AND AVOCADO BLEU CHEESE SANDWICH

8 ounces Bleu cheese
2 tablespoons mayonnaise
1 tablespoon milk

12 slices bacon, fried crisp
8 slices whole-wheat toast
1 avocado, peeled and sliced

Using food processor, mix cheese, mayonnaise and milk. Fold in four pieces of crumbled bacon until spreadable. Spread on all slices of wheat toast. Place bacon strips and avocado slices on the top. Combine the slices to make four sandwiches.

Serves: four.

$\mathcal{H}$OT PESTO PROSCIUTTO SANDWICH

1 loaf Italian bread
1 cup mayonnaise
1/2 cup pesto
1/2 pound sliced prosciutto

8 ounces Provolone cheese, sliced
1 small onion, thinly sliced

Slice the bread lengthwise. Mix mayonnaise and pesto. Spread on the bread. Layer with prosciutto and cheese. Top with onion. Broil open-faced until hot and bubbly.

Serves: four to six.

Atlantic Beach Hotel.
Photograph is from collections at The Beaches Area Historical Society Archives.

Breads & Pastries

The downtown skyline is both dramatic and enticing whether leisurely being seen from a boat or viewing form the Southbank River Walk.

The old St. Johns Lighthouse is the oldest building in Mayport, being built in 1858. Two earlier lighthouses were abandoned and removed due to their perilous proximity to the ocean.

Photograph is from collections at The Beaches Area Historical Society.

RIVER CITY ROLLS

2 packages dry yeast	1 cup warm water
3 tablespoons warm water	4 to 4 1/2 cups flour, divided
1/2 cup sugar	1/4 cup plus 2 tablespoons
1/2 cup butter, melted	butter
2 eggs, beaten	

Dissolve yeast in three tablespoons warm water in large mixing bowl. Let stand five minutes. Add sugar, butter, eggs, one cup warm water, salt and two cups flour. Beat at low speed of electric mixer one minute. Gradually stir in enough remaining flour to make soft dough. Turn dough out onto lightly floured surface; knead four minutes or until smooth and elastic. Shape dough into a ball and place in a well greased bowl, turning to grease top. Cover and let rise for one hour or until doubled in bulk. Punch dough down and divide into four equal parts. Roll each into a 12-inch circle on a floured surface; brush with butter. Cut each circle into six wedges; roll up each wedge, beginning at wide end. Place on baking sheets, point side down, pushing tip down on baking sheet. Cover and let rise for one hour or until doubled in bulk. Preheat oven to 400°. Bake for eight to 10 minutes. Brush warm rolls with any remaining butter.

These rolls are extra special, as my friend Ann assured me. Once I made them, I was hooked. They are delicious at a brunch and equally good at a holiday table. They also freeze beautifully.

Yield: four dozen.

"My sister has always lovingly been called the dough girl, partly because she was such a chubby little child and partly because at an early age she could make the most wonderful yeast rolls! One Christmas Eve is quite memorable. When we walked down the hall filled with the aroma of yeast rolls, we found Kathy flopping around on the floor in front of the fireplace. It seems, she had lit the gas jet and flames had singed her eyebrows and nose hairs! Thankfully, she was not hurt and served her rolls without missing a beat. The memory of the rest of the meal fails me now, but I do remember how we all bragged and bragged on the rolls made by my pitiful singed sister."

CHALLAH

2 cups milk
1/2 cup butter, divided
1/3 cup sugar
2 packages dry yeast
4 eggs, room temperature

2 teaspoons salt
6 cups flour
1/3 cup cornmeal
1 tablespoon cold water

Bring milk, six tablespoons of the butter and the sugar to a boil in medium size saucepan. Remove from heat, pour into large mixing bowl and cool to lukewarm (105° to 115°). Stir yeast into milk mixture and let stand for 10 minutes. Beat three of the eggs well in a small bowl, and stir them and the salt into the milk/yeast mixture. Stir in five cups of flour, one cup at a time. Achieve a sticky dough. Flour a work surface lightly and turn the dough out onto it. Wash and dry the bowl. Sprinkle additional flour over the dough and begin kneading, adding more flour as necessary, until you have a smooth elastic dough. Grease the inside of the bowl with the reserved two tablespoons butter and add ball of dough. Cover bowl with towel and set aside until dough is tripled in bulk one and one-half to two hours. Turn dough onto lightly floured work surface and cut in half. Cut each half into three pieces. Roll pieces out onto long snakes at 18-inches long. Braid three snakes into a loaf and tuck ends under. Repeat with remaining snakes. Sprinkle a large baking sheet with cornmeal and transfer the loaves to the sheet. Leave room between the loaves for them to rise. Cover loaves with the towel and let rise until nearly doubled, about one hour. Preheat oven to 350°. Beat the remaining egg and one tablespoon cold water together well in a small bowl. Brush this egg wash evenly over the loaves. Sit baking sheet on the middle rack of the oven. Bake 30-35 minutes, or until loaves are golden brown and sound hollow when their bottoms are thumped. Cool completely on racks.

Yield: two loaves.

Challah is a traditional Jewish bread. When served on the Sabbath Challah is generally braided. Although it is highly unlikely that you will have any of this delicious bread leftover, it is perfect in bread pudding.

OCACCIA

1/4 ounce package dry yeast
1 cup warm water
2 3/4 cups bread flour
3 tablespoons whole wheat
  flour
4 tablespoons olive oil,
  divided
2 teaspoons table salt

1 tablespoon minced garlic, or
  to taste
2 tablespoons minced fresh
  basil
2 tablespoons minced fresh
  oregano
kosher salt to taste

Sprinkle yeast in water for five minutes or until foamy. In large bowl stir together the flours, two tablespoons of the oil, the table salt, and the yeast mixture, turn the dough out onto a lightly floured surface and knead for eight to 10 minutes, or until it is smooth and elastic. Transfer dough to a lightly oiled bowl, turning it to coat it well, and let it rise for one hour or until doubled in bulk. Preheat oven to 375°. With the finger-tips, press the dough into a well-oiled 16-x 12-inch jelly roll pan. Brush the dough with the remaining two tablespoons oil and sprinkle it with the garlic, herbs and the kosher salt. Bake the focaccia in the middle of a oven for 20 or 30 minutes or until it is golden and brush with additional olive oil. Cut into two inch squares.

Focaccia, a fragrant bread similar to pizza dough, is rising in popularity. Traditionally, olive oil and salt are drizzled into finger-marked wells on focaccia, allowing the flavor to seep into the bread. Try preparing these focaccia recipes in several ways; smear them with soft, herbed cheese; filling it with eggplant, onion and provolone cheese, and serving with olive oil.

Yield: 48 squares.

"That's the beauty of making bread. You can spend one day baking and reap the rewards for weeks. It's wonderfully Old World."

DRIED TOMATO FOCACCIA

1/3 cup minced dried
  tomatoes
1/2 cup boiling water
1 cup milk
2 tablespoons butter
3 1/2 to 4 cups bread flour,
  divided
2 packages active dried yeast

2 tablespoons sugar
2 teaspoons salt
1 large egg
3 tablespoons diced chives
1/4 cup olive oil
1/4 teaspoon dried oregano
1/4 teaspoon dried rosemary

Combine tomatoes and boiling water in a small saucepan; let stand 25 minutes. Remove tomatoes, reserving liquid; set aside. Stir milk and butter into reserve liquid. Heat until mixture reaches 120° to 130°. Combine one and one-half cups flour, yeast, sugar and salt in large mixing bowl. Gradually add liquid mixture to flour mixture, beating at low speed with an electric mixer. Add egg, and beat three minutes at medium speed. Stir in tomatoes, chives and enough remaining flour to make a soft dough. Turn dough out onto floured surface, and knead five minutes. Place in a well greased bowl, cover and let rise in warm place one hour or until doubled in bulk. Combine olive oil, oregano and rosemary; set aside. Punch dough down. Preheat oven to 350°. For round loaves, divide dough in half; shape each portion into 10-inch round. Place on lightly greased baking sheets; flatten dough slightly and brush with half of olive oil mixture period. Cover and let rest 10 minutes. Bake for 15 minutes. Brush with remaining olive oil mixture and bake extra five to 10 minutes or until lightly browned. Cool on wire racks.

Yield: two 10-inch loaves.

"My mother always used to say that even a first time baker can make better bread than she could buy."

JULIE'S ONE HOUR BAGUETTE

1 1/2 cups warm water
1 1/2 tablespoons yeast
1 tablespoon honey
2 cups white flour
2 cups wheat flour
1 teaspoon salt

6 tablespoons mixed fresh
  herbs (thyme, rosemary, sage
  and basil) or 3 1/2 teaspoons dried
1 cup grated Cheddar, Provolone, Parmesan or Monterey
  Jack cheese
olive oil

Combine the warm water, yeast and honey in a large bowl. Let sit in a warm spot for 10-15 minutes or until the yeast has dissolved and starts to bubble. Sift the flours and salt over the yeast mixture, one cup at a time, and mix until the dough forms a large ball. Use the dough attachment on a food processor and mix after each cup of flour is added. Lightly flour a work surface and a rolling pin. Cut dough in half and roll each half out to form a rectangle about 15-inches long and eight inches wide. Scatter half the herbs and cheeses over the surface of one rectangle, and lightly press them into the dough. Roll up the dough gently into the shape of a baguette. Repeat with the other half of the dough. Place in a well greased french bread pan or on a cookie sheet. Drape a clean tea towel over the dough and set in a warm spot for 20 minutes to rise. Preheat oven to 450°. Lightly brush the loaves with olive oil and bake for 20 minutes on the middle rack. Remove and let cool slightly before serving. Cool for one hour before freezing.

Great for parties because it can be made well in advance and frozen. Other combinations of wheat and white flour may be used, but this combination is the tastiest!

Yield: two baguettes.

CHUNKY CHOCOLATE CHERRY BREAD

3/4 cup milk
1/2 cup butter
1/4 cup sugar
1 package dry yeast
1/4 cup warm water
3 to 3 1/2 cups flour,
   divided
3 tablespoons cocoa
3/4 teaspoon salt

1/8 teaspoon ground
   cinnamon
2 eggs
2 teaspoons vanilla
1/2 cup semisweet chocolate
   chunks
1 cup dried cherries
Glaze (recipe follows)

Combine three-quarters cup milk, butter, and sugar in sauce-pan; heat until butter melts. Cool to 105° to 115°. Dissolve yeast in warm water in a large mixing bowl. Let stand five minutes. Add butter mixture, two cups flour, cocoa, salt, cinnamon, eggs and vanilla. Beat at low speed of an electric mixer 30 seconds. Beat an additional three minutes at medium speed. Gradually stir in enough remaining flour to make a soft dough. Turn dough out onto a floured surface and knead until smooth and elastic (about eight to 10 minutes). Place in a well-greased bowl, turning to grease top. Cover and let rise in a warm place (85°), free from drafts, one hour or until doubled in bulk. Punch down and turn out onto a floured surface. Roll into an 18- by 10-inch rectangle. Sprinkle with chocolate chunks and dried cherries, pressing chunks gently into dough. Roll up dough, jellyroll fashion, starting at one short end. Fold ends under and place seam side down in a greased 9-by 5- by 3-inch loaf pan. Cover and let rise in a warm place, free from drafts, for 45 minutes or until loaf has doubled in bulk. Heat oven to 350° and bake for 30 minutes or until loaf sounds hollow when tapped. Remove bread from pan immediately; cool on a wire rack. Drizzle glaze over loaf.

Glaze
1 cup sifted powder sugar
1 1/2 tablespoons milk

1/2 teaspoon vanilla

Combine all ingredients, stirring well.

Yield: one loaf.

MAPLE OATMEAL BREAD

1 envelope dry yeast
1 1/4 teaspoons sugar
2/3 cup warm water
2 1/2 cups flour
1/2 cup wheat flour
1/3 cup cooked oatmeal

1/3 plus 1/2 cup maple syrup
1/4 cup milk
2 tablespoons butter, softened
1 teaspoon salt

Combine yeast and sugar with warm water in small bowl. Let stand 10 minutes. Blend with mixer flours, oatmeal, syrup, milk, butter and salt. Add yeast mixture. Remove to lightly floured surface and knead 10 times. Place dough in lightly greased bowl and cover. Let rise until doubled in bulk, about one hour. Transfer dough to lightly floured surface and roll into rectangle. Roll up lengthwise. Pinch ends and seam together lightly. Place loaf, seam-side down in an oiled 5- by 9-inch loaf pan sprinkled with oatmeal. Fold ends under if necessary to fit pan. Let stand again for 45 minutes. Bake at 375° for 35 to 45 minutes or until loaf is golden. Glaze with maple syrup.

Here in the South we tend to think of maple syrup, that delectable treat from the north, only at breakfast. You'll want to serve this bread any time during the day and for dinner, too.

Yield: one loaf.

"Only a home cook would take the time to brush homemade rolls with melted butter before and after they're in the oven."

GLAZED ORANGE ROLLS

1 package dry yeast
3/4 cup warm water (105° to 115°)
3 to 3 1/4 cups flour, divided
3 tablespoons sugar
1 1/2 teaspoons salt
1 egg
2 tablespoons butter or margarine, melted
1 tablespoon grated orange rind
1/4 cup orange juice
1 orange, peeled, sectioned, and chopped
1 tablespoon sugar
Orange Butter Glaze (recipe follows)

Dissolve yeast in warm water in a large bowl. Let stand five minutes. Add one cup flour, sugar, salt, egg, butter, orange rind and orange juice. Beat at medium speed until well blended. Gradually stir in enough remaining flour to make a soft dough. Turn dough out on well floured surface, and knead until smooth (about five minutes). Place in a well greased bowl, turning to grease top. Cover and let rise in warm place until doubled in bulk. Punch dough down; turn out onto a lightly floured surface, and knead lightly five times. Roll dough to one-quarter inch thickness; cut with two and one-half inch biscuit cutter. Cover with towel and let stand 20 minutes. Combine chopped orange and one tablespoon sugar. Let stand five minutes. Drain and pat dry between paper towels; set aside. Make a crease across each circle, and place an orange piece in center. Fold over; gently press edges to seal. Place rolls in lightly greased 13- by 9- by 2-inch baking pan. Cover and let rise 30 minutes. Heat oven to 425° and bake for 15 minutes. Spread with glaze.

Orange Butter Glaze
1 tablespoon butter, softened
1 teaspoon grated orange rind
1 1/4 cup sifted powder sugar
1 3/4 tablespoons orange juice
1 1/2 teaspoons lemon juice

Cream butter and orange juice; add powdered sugar and orange rind alternately with juices, beating until blended.

Yield: two dozen rolls.

HOT CROSS BUNS

3 1/2 to 4 cups flour, divided
2 packages active dry yeast
1/4 teaspoon dried ground
  cloves
1 teaspoon cinnamon
3/4 cup milk
1/2 cup oil
1/3 cup granulated sugar
1/2 teaspoon salt
3 eggs
2/3 cup dried currants
1 egg white
1 1/2 cups sifted powdered
  sugar
1/2 teaspoon vanilla

Combine one and one-half cups of the flour, yeast, cloves and cinnamon in large mixing bowl; set aside. Heat milk, oil, granulated sugar and salt in a saucepan just until warm; stirring constantly. Add to flour mixture then add eggs. Beat at low speed of electric mixer for one minute, scraping sides of bowl constantly. Stir in currents and as much of the remaining flour that you can mix in with a spoon. Turn dough out onto a lightly floured surface. Knead in enough of the remaining flour to make a soft dough that is smooth and elastic. Shape into a ball. Place in a lightly greased bowl; turn once to grease surface. Cover; let rise in a warm place until double, about one hour. Punch down; turn out onto floured surface. Cover, let rest for 10 minutes. Divide dough into 18 pieces; form each piece into a smooth ball. Place on a greased baking sheet one and one-half inches apart. Cover; let rise 30 to 45 minutes. Heat oven to 375°. Cut a shallow cross with a sharp knife into each bun. Brush tops with some of the beaten egg white. Bake for 12 to 15 minutes or until golden. Cool slightly. Meanwhile, combine powdered sugar and vanilla. Add additional milk, if necessary, to make a piping consistency. Pipe crosses on tops of buns.

Try adding finely minced dried apricots and cherries to the dough for an tasty variation.

Yield: 18 buns.

POPOVERS

4 eggs	1 1/2 cups milk
1 cup flour	2 tablespoons butter, melted
pinch salt	

Preheat oven to 400°. Mix eggs with flour and salt. Beat well. Mix milk and butter into flour mixture until smooth. Grease muffin tins with melted butter. Fill greased muffin tin cups two-thirds full. Bake 35 minutes.

Popovers should be crisp, golden brown and shiny on the outside and soft and tender on the inside. We love popovers with butter and honey or jelly. Serve them also with roast beef and pork.

Yield: 12 popovers.

CINNAMON POPOVERS

3 eggs, beaten well	1/8 teaspoon salt
1 cup flour	1 cup milk
1 tablespoon sugar	3 tablespoons melted butter or
1 teaspoon ground cinnamon	margarine

Preheat oven to 425°. Combine all ingredients and mix well with electric mixer. Grease muffin tins with melted butter. Place well-greased muffin tins in oven three minutes. Remove pans from oven. Fill each muffin cup one-half full with batter. Bake for 15 minutes. Reduce heat to 350° and bake an additional 12 - 15 minutes or until popovers are firm and puffed. Serve immediately.

Yield: one dozen.

"The Little House on the Prairie books were my absolute favorite as a child. I would read about Laura's Ma making cornbread in a skillet over a fire and nothing would do for me until I had pestered my mother into making some cornbread."

$\mathscr{B}$ACON CHEDDAR CORNBREAD

1 1/2 cups flour
1 1/2 cups cornmeal
3 tablespoons sugar
4 teaspoons baking powder
1/4 teaspoon salt
1 1/2 cups milk

1/2 cup oil
1 egg, slightly beaten
6 strips bacon, cooked and
  crumbled
1 cup shredded Cheddar
  cheese

Heat oven to 375°. Grease four 5 1/2- by 3-inch loaf pans. Combine flour, cornmeal, sugar, baking powder and salt in a medium bowl. Mix well. Stir in remaining ingredients just until smooth. Pour batter into prepared pans. Bake for 40–45 minutes or until toothpick comes out clean.

Cornbread belongs in a category all its own. It is a staple in our kitchens today as it has been in the South for generations. Cornbread is easy to prepare and is a natural accompaniment for salads, soups, chilies and fish. This recipe is a different take on an old favorite.

Yield: four small loaves.

$\mathscr{C}$ORNBREAD

2 eggs
5 tablespoons sugar
1/2 cup butter, melted
1 cup flour
2 teaspoons baking powder

1/2 teaspoon baking soda
3/4 teaspoon salt
2/3 cup yellow cornmeal
1 cup buttermilk

Preheat oven to 400°. Beat eggs and add sugar. Mix in melted butter. Sift together flour, baking soda, baking powder, salt and cornmeal. Alternately add dry and wet ingredients with buttermilk. Pour batter into buttered, nine inch round pan. Bake 30 minutes.

Serves: eight.

VIRGINIA SPOON BREAD

2 cups milk
3/4 cup white cornmeal
3 eggs, separated

1 teaspoon salt
4 tablespoons butter

Preheat oven to 350°. Heat milk in heavy pan, stirring frequently to prevent scorching. Stir cornmeal in slowly. Add butter and salt and let cool. Beat in egg yolks. Beat egg whites until stiff then fold into batter. Pour into buttered dish and bake 30 minutes.

Yield: four to six servings.

Spoon bread is a southern bread that is similar to a souffle but is not as fragile or light. The bread is brought to the table straight from the oven and spooned onto the plates. Delicious with ham and red eye gravy, roast chicken and gravy, or roast pork and gravy. It is also yummy with honey or molasses.

NEW ORLEANS STYLE FRENCH LOAF

1 large loaf French bread
3/4 cup unsalted butter,
  softened
1 teaspoon dried thyme

1/2 teaspoon hot pepper sauce
1/2 cup sliced red onions
2 cups grated sharp Cheddar
  cheese

Preheat oven to 400°. Cut the bread lengthwise. Beat the butter with the thyme and hot pepper sauce then spread mixture on both sides inside the loaf. Lay the onions on the bottom slice and sprinkle evenly with cheese. Top with the other slice and wrap securely with foil. Bake for 20 to 25 minutes or until crust is hard. Slice crosswise to serve.

The touch of thyme in this recipe accents the sharp cheese and the bite of the red onions nicely.

Serves: eight.

SWEET POTATO BISCUITS

3/4 cup cooked mashed sweet
potatoes
4 tablespoons butter, melted
2/3 cup milk
1 1/4 cup flour

2 1/2 teaspoons baking
powder
1 tablespoon sugar
1/2 teaspoon salt

Heat oven to 425°. Beat butter into mashed sweet potatoes.
Stir in milk and set aside. Mix flour, baking powder, sugar
and salt, stirring well. Stir dry ingredients into sweet potato
mixture. Turn dough out on a floured surface and knead
lightly until it is smooth on the outside. Roll or pat it to the
thickness one-half inch. Cut with floured biscuit cutter. Bake
on well-greased baking sheet for 15 minutes.

Yield: 20 biscuits.

*Sweet potatoes embody the flavor and essence of Southern cooking.
Reminiscent of good foods in tranquil surroundings, the sweet potato
has long been revered in the South as one of the finest vegetables.*

*As a child, I was fascinated by my mother's poise. Every day she
would create a delicious breakfast while wearing a cheerful robe; her
makeup perfectly set. She'd hum to the radio as the aromas from her
kitchen would meander through the house. This was 5:30 a.m. in the
morning, mind you. I was in awe.*

*One day, while I was sleepily helping her, the timer went off from
some biscuits that were browning in the oven. Calmly, my mother
donned an oven mitt and picked up the phone. "Hello." Not until
she repeated her salutation and still received no reply did she realize
what had occurred. Shaking her head and smiling in self-amuse-
ment, she hung up the phone and took the biscuits out of the oven.
Not only did my mother have poise, she also had charm and grace.*

ANTIPASTO BREAD

1 large loaf French bread
1/2 cup butter
1/4 cup olive oil
10 large cloves of garlic, chopped and peeled
1 10 ounce package chopped spinach, thawed and squeezed
1 14 ounce can artichoke hearts, drained and chopped

1/2 cup chopped parsley
8 anchovy fillets, finely cut
1 cup Swiss cheese, grated
1/2 cup grated mozzarella
3 tablespoons capers
1 teaspoon pepper
pinch of dried tarragon and basil

Heat oven to 350°. Cut off one-quarter top of loaf, cutting lengthwise. Scoop out inside of loaf carefully then tearing it into small pieces. Place pieces in a large mixing bowl. Melt butter and oil in large skillet, add garlic. Saute´ 60 seconds. Add spinach, artichoke hearts, parsley and anchovies. Toss well on medium heat for 10 minutes. Add to bread pieces; stir in cheeses, capers, pepper and herbs. When mixed well, pack mixture into bread hollow. Replace top and wrap in foil. Bake 30 minutes. Unwrap and brush with olive oil. Bake five more minutes. Unwrap and let sit for 10 minutes. Slice into one and one-half inch pieces. Serve warm.

Yield: one loaf, serves 10 to 12.

Casper and Ida Beerbower on Challen and Riverside.
Photograph is from collections at The Riverside/Avondale Preservation Archives.

$\mathscr{G}$RILLED BREAKFAST SANDWICHES

3 tablespoons orange juice
1 egg
4 ounces thinly sliced deli
  ham

4 slices cinnamon raisin bread
vegetable cooking spray
1 teaspoon powdered sugar
2 tablespoons jelly or jam

Combine orange juice and egg in a shallow bowl. Beat with a wire whisk and set aside. Place two ham slices on each of two cinnamon raisin bread slices and top with remaining bread. Coat a large skillet with cooking spray, and place over medium heat until hot. Dip each sandwich into egg mixture, coating well. Cook sandwiches three minutes on each side or until golden. Sift powdered sugar over sandwiches. Serve sandwiches with jam.

There are many good reasons to get out of bed in the morning and among the best of them is the anticipation of breakfast. These breakfast sandwiches are little trouble and such a treat.

Yield: two sandwiches.

OTATO BACON BISCUITS

1/2 cup butter or margarine
1 cup instant potato flakes
3/4 cup buttermilk
8 slices bacon, cooked and
  crumbled

1/2 cup shredded colby
  cheese
melted butter or margarine

Preheat oven to 425°. Cut one-half cup butter into potato flakes with a pastry blender until mixture is crumbly. Add buttermilk, stirring until dry ingredients are moist. Add bacon and cheese. Turn dough out onto lightly floured surface. Knead three or four times. Roll dough to three-quarter inch thickness. Cut with a two and one-half inch, round cutter and place onto baking sheet. Bake 12-14 minutes. Brush with melted butter.

Serves: eight.

MACADAMIA FRENCH TOAST (OVERNIGHT)

6 eggs
1/2 cup milk
1/4 teaspoon ground nut-
  meg
1 cup orange juice
1/3 cup sugar
1 teaspoon vanilla

1 16-inch loaf French bread,
  cut into 1 inch slices
1/3 cup butter
1/2 cup chopped macadamia
  nuts
cream of coconut

Beat eggs, milk, nutmeg, orange juice, sugar and vanilla with wire whisk. Place bread slices in two 13- by 9- inch cake pans. Pour half of egg mixture in each pan over bread; cover tightly. Refrigerate overnight. All the egg mixture will be absorbed. Preheat oven to 400°. Melt butter; and divide between two jelly roll pans. Place soaked bread slices, without sides touching on buttered pans. Sprinkle with nuts. Bake 20 to 25 minutes, or until golden brown. Serve with cream of coconut.

Wonderful tasting with a special flavor twist of macadamia nuts and cream of coconut. It resembles a traditional type of French toast, but with less last-minute preparation. The bottom of the toast is a golden brown with a crisp lightly browned top crust. Cream of coconut is available in cans in most supermarkets.

Serves: eight.

View at Riverside.
Photograph is from collections at The Jacksonville Historical Society Archives.

GERMAN APPLE PANCAKES

1 cup milk
3 large eggs, beaten
3/4 cup flour
3 tablespoons sugar, divided
2 tablespoons butter
2 medium cooking apples like
  Granny Smith, peeled, cored
  and cut into 1/4 inch slices

1/4 teaspoon cinnamon
1 tablespoon confectioners'
  sugar
lemon wedges, optional

Heat oven to 375°. In medium-size bowl, whisk together milk, eggs, flour and two tablespoons sugar. Melt butter in 9- or 10-inch heavy ovenproof skillet over medium-high heat. Add apples, cinnamon and remaining one tablespoon sugar. Reduce heat to medium and cook, stirring occasionally, for two to three minutes, or until apples are softened slightly. Remove pan from heat. Pour batter over apples in pan. Place pan in oven and bake for 35 to 40 minutes, or until pancake is lightly browned and puffy. Remove pan from oven and cut pancake into wedges. Transfer wedges to warmed serving plates, dust wedges with confectioners' sugar and serve with lemon if desired.

Serves: six to eight.

"We used to make these pancakes on Saturday night. They were such a special treat. I can still smell the apples cooking."

ORTEGA'S BEST SOUR CREAM COFFEE CAKE

<u>Almond Filling</u>
1 package (3 1/2 oz.)
  almond paste
1/2 cup powdered sugar

1/4 cup butter or margarine
1/2 cup almonds

Heat cut up almond paste, powdered sugar and butter or margarine over medium heat, stirring constantly until smooth. Stir in almonds. Reserve.

<u>Batter</u>
1 1/2 cups sugar
3/4 cup butter or
  margarine, softened
1 1/2 teaspoons vanilla
3 eggs
3 cups flour

1 1/2 teaspoons baking
  powder
1 1/2 teaspoons baking soda
3/4 teaspoon salt
1 1/2 cups sour cream

Preheat oven to 325°. Beat sugar, butter, vanilla and eggs on medium for two minutes. Beat in flour, baking powder, baking soda and salt alternately with sour cream on low speed. Spread one-third of batter (about two cups) into greased tube pan. Sprinkle with one-third of the filling. Repeat two times. Bake one hour. Let cool for 20 minutes.

<u>Glaze</u>
1/2 cup powdered sugar

1/4 teaspoon vanilla
1-2 teaspoons milk

Mix all ingredients together until smooth. Remove cake from pan and glaze.

I had forgotten how delicious this coffee cake is warm and fresh from the oven. It reminds me of the coffee cakes my mother used to make.

Yield: one cake.

RING'S POPPY SEED BREAD

3 cups flour
1 1/2 teaspoons salt
2 1/4 cups sugar
1 1/3 tablespoons poppy
  seeds
1 1/2 teaspoons baking
  powder
3 eggs

1 1/2 cups milk
1 1/8 cups oil
1 1/2 teaspoons vanilla
1 1/2 teaspoons almond
  flavoring
1 1/2 teaspoons butter
  flavoring

Preheat oven to 350°. Mix all ingredients two minutes with electric mixer on medium speed. Pour into three lightly-oiled loaf pans (8 1/2-by 4 1/2-by 2 1/2-inches). Bake one hour. Allow to cool 10 minutes before glazing.

Glaze

1/4 cup orange juice
3/4 cup sugar
1/2 teaspoon vanilla

1/2 teaspoon almond
flavoring
1/2 teaspoon butter flavoring

Heat all ingredients together until sugar dissolves. Brush or pour glaze over warm cakes.

This bread is so delicious - it is really like a pound cake. It is great for teacher presents. Poppy seed bread makes a gift that is always received with great enthusiasm.

Yield: three loaves.

STRAWBERRY BREAD
With Cream Cheese Spread

3 cups flour
2 cups sugar
1 teaspoon baking soda
1 teaspoon cinnamon
1/2 teaspoon salt
1 cup strawberry juice,
  divided

2 10-ounce packages frozen
  strawberries, thawed and
  chopped
1 cup oil
4 eggs, well beaten

Heat oven to 350°. Combine and mix well flour, sugar, baking soda, cinnamon and salt. Make a well in center and add one-half cup strawberry juice, strawberries, oil and eggs. Mix by hand. Grease and flour two 4- by 8-inch loaf pans. Bake for one hour or until toothpick inserted in center comes out clean.

Cream Cheese Spread
8 ounces cream cheese,
  softened

strawberry juice

Combine cream cheese with enough strawberry juice to make a spreadable mixture. Spread on bread and refrigerate until served.

Loaves can be frozen. Sliced them thinly before they are completely thawed.

Yield: two loaves.

"Ever since my children have been old enough to play patty cake and bake pretend cakes in their play kitchens, they have loved helping me bake."

BLUEBERRY LEMON BREAD

1 1/2 cups flour
1 teaspoon baking powder
1/4 teaspoon salt
6 tablespoons unsalted
  butter, room
  temperature
1 1/3 cups sugar, divided
2 large eggs

2 teaspoons grated lemon peel
1/2 cup milk
1 1/2 cups fresh blueberries
  (or frozen: thawed and
  drained)
3 tablespoons fresh lemon
  juice

Preheat oven to 325°. Butter 8 1/2- by 4 1/2- by 2 1/2-inch loaf pan. Combine flour, baking powder and salt in small bowl. Using electric mixer, cream butter with one cup sugar in large bowl until mixture is light and fluffy. Add eggs one at a time, beating well after each addition. Add lemon peel. Mix in dry ingredients alternately with milk, beginning and ending with dry ingredients. Fold in blueberries. Spoon batter into prepared loaf pan. Bake until golden brown and toothpick inserted into center comes out clean, about one hour 15 minutes. Meanwhile, bring remaining one-third cup sugar and lemon juice to boil in small saucepan, stirring until sugar dissolves. Pierce top of hot loaf several times with toothpick. Pour hot lemon mixture over loaf in pan. Cool 30 minutes in pan on rack. Turn bread out of pan and cool completely on rack.

Yield: one loaf.

DUTCH APPLE BREAD

1 cup sugar
1/2 cup butter
2 eggs, beaten
2 cups sifted flour
1 teaspoon baking soda
1/4 teaspoon salt
1 1/2 tablespoon sour milk

1 teaspoon vanilla
1 tablespoon orange juice
1 cup peeled and chopped
   apples
1 teaspoon cinnamon
2 tablespoons brown sugar

Preheat oven to 350°. Cream sugar and butter. Add eggs. Sift flour, baking soda and salt then add to egg mixture. Add milk, vanilla, orange juice and apples. Grease two small or one large loaf pan. Sprinkle cinnamon and brown sugar on top. Bake 50-60 minutes.

Yield: one large or two small loaves.

A cottage on the site of the Woman's Club of Jacksonville on Riverside Ave.
Photograph is from collections at The Jacksonville Historical Society Archives.

"As I regularly sit down to a bowl of cereal each morning, I am reminded of the funny things that my parents ate for breakfast. Often my mother would be found seated at the foot of the stairs eating whatever she hadn't found room for the night before. A quartered watermelon seemed to be one of her favorites. Poached fish was much enjoyed by my father for breakfast."

GINGERBREAD
With Lemon-Orange Sauce

Batter

1 2/3 cups flour	1 egg, beaten
1 1/4 teaspoons baking soda	1/2 cup sugar
3/4 teaspoon ground ginger	1/2 cup molasses
3/4 teaspoon ground cinnamon	1/2 cup boiling water
1/2 teaspoon salt	1/2 cup oil
1/4 teaspoon ground cloves	

Preheat oven to 350° and grease nine-inch square pan. Sift flour, baking soda, ginger, cinnamon, salt and cloves into bowl. Add eggs, sugar and molasses. Mix well. Pour boiling water and oil over mixture. Stir until smooth. Bake for 35-40 minutes until edges pull away from sides.

Glaze

2/3 cup powdered sugar	2 tablespoons orange juice
2 tablespoons lemon juice	

Sift sugar into bowl and add juices and mix well. While gingerbread is still hot, pour glaze over top. Cool in pan.

Serve this piping hot for a special dessert with the wonderfully tangy lemon- orange sauce.

Yield: one nine inch square.

Old-fashioned gingerbread, that spicy cake-like delicacy has been with us for generations. Even William Shakespeare paid tribute to it: "Had I but one penny in the world, thou shouldst have it for gingerbread." Love's Labor's Lost.

𝒫EANUT BUTTER CHOCOLATE CHIP BREAD

3 cups flour
1 1/2 teaspoons baking powder
1 teaspoon baking soda
1/2 teaspoon salt
6 tablespoons unsalted butter, softened
1 1/2 cups chunk-style peanut butter

1 cup firmly packed brown sugar
2 large eggs
1 1/4 cups buttermilk
1 3/4 cups miniature chocolate chips

Preheat oven to 350°. Sift together flour, baking powder, baking soda and salt. Cream together in a separate bowl with an electric mixer butter, peanut butter and brown sugar. Beat in the eggs, one at a time. Add buttermilk and beat until the mixture is combined well. Add the flour mixture and beat the batter just until combined, then stir in the chocolate chips. Divide the batter among five buttered and floured loaf pans, each 5 1/4- by 3 1/4- by 2-inches, and bake the breads in the middle of oven for 40 to 45 minutes or until a tester comes out clean. Remove the breads from the pans and let them cool right side up on a rack. The breads keep, well wrapped, chilled for one week or frozen for one month.

Yield: five loaves.

Oranges were introduced to Florida by the Spanish, who planted groves of sour oranges around Orange and Lochloosa Lakes in Central North Florida. The Indians may have roasted the sour oranges over their outdoor fires. Southern Ladies gathered the oranges to make a refreshing drink for the soldiers during the Civil War. It's hard to imagine a cookbook from Florida without a "gracious plenty" of orange recipes.

ORANGE-RAISIN BRAN MUFFINS

2 1/2 cups flour
1 cup bran cereal
1 cup sugar
1 1/2 teaspoons baking soda
1 teaspoons salt

2 eggs, beaten
1 1/2 cup buttermilk
1/2 cup oil
1/2 orange juice concentrate
1 cup raisins

Stir flour, cereal, sugar, baking soda and salt together. Mix eggs, buttermilk, oil and orange juice with electric mixer at medium speed until well blended. Make a well in dry ingredients mixture. Pour in wet mixture and stir thoroughly. Add raisins. Refrigerate batter overnight. Bring to room temperature and spoon into muffin tins. Bake in preheated 400° oven for 20 minutes.

Makes 24 muffins.

DRIED CHERRY MUFFINS

1/2 cup unsalted butter,
  softened
3/4 cup sugar
2 large eggs
2 teaspoons grated lemon rind
2 tablespoons lemon juice
2 cups flour

1 teaspoon baking soda
1/2 teaspoon salt
1 cup buttermilk
2/3 cup chopped dried
  cherries
1/2 cup chopped walnuts

Preheat oven to 400°. Beat butter at medium speed with electric mixer until creamy. Add sugar gradually, and beat well. Add eggs, one at a time, beating after each addition. Stir in lemon rind and lemon juice. Combine flour, soda and salt. Add to butter mixture alternately, with buttermilk, beginning and ending with flour mixture. Stir just until blended. Stir in cherries and walnuts. Spoon into greased muffin tins. Bake 20 minutes.

Yield: 15 muffins.

ℬUTTERMILK ORANGE MUFFINS
With Fresh Orange Sauce

1/2 cup butter, softened
1 cup sugar
2 eggs
1 teaspoon baking soda

2 cups flour
1/4 teaspoon salt
2/3 cup buttermilk

Preheat oven to 375°. Cream butter and sugar. Add eggs, one at a time. Sift baking soda, flour and salt then add alternately with the buttermilk to the sugar mixture. Spoon into greased miniature muffin tins, about one-half full. Bake for 10-12 minutes. Do not overcook.

Orange Sauce
juice from two oranges

grated rind from one orange
1 cup sugar

Simmer ingredients over low heat until sugar is dissolved. Spoon one teaspoon sauce over each muffin while they are warm and still in the pan. Allow to cool in the tins. Then remove and store in covered container in the refrigerator.

Yield: about 78 mini-muffins.

Traditionally made fresh in a churn, buttermilk adds a rich flavor to delicious, old-fashioned bread and muffins.

𝒞HEDDAR RAISIN MUFFINS

2 cups flour
3 1/2 teaspoons baking powder
1/2 teaspoon salt
1/4 teaspoon paprika
1/4 cup butter

1 cup shredded cheddar
   cheese
2/3 cup raisins
1 cup milk
1 large egg, beaten

Heat oven to 425°. Combine flour, baking powder, salt and paprika. Cut in butter until resembles a coarse mixture. Stir in cheese and raisins. Spoon into greased muffin tins. Make a well in the center of the batter and add milk and egg. Bake 20 to 25 minutes.
Yield: 12-14 muffins.

PUMPKIN-CHOCOLATE CHIP MUFFINS

1/2 cup sliced unblanched
  almonds
1 2/3 cups flour
1 cup sugar
1 tablespoon pumpkin pie
  spice
1 teaspoon baking soda

1/4 teaspoon baking powder
1/4 teaspoon salt
2 large eggs
1 cup plain pumpkin (one-
  half of one pound can)
1/2 cup butter, melted
1 cup chocolate chips

Preheat oven to 350°. Put almonds on baking sheet and bake until just lightly brown (approximately five minutes). Let cool. Grease muffin cups or use paper baking cups. Mix flour, sugar, pumpkin pie spice, baking soda, baking powder and salt in a large bowl. Combine eggs, pumpkin and butter. Whisk mixture until well blended. Stir in chocolate chips and almonds. Pour over dry ingredients and mix until just moistened. Spoon batter into muffin cups. Bake 20-25 minutes.

Best if prepared one to two days in advance. Reheat before serving.

Yield: 12 muffins.

AVONDALE CINNAMON SUGAR MUFFINS

1 1/2 cup flour
2 teaspoons baking soda
1/4 teaspoon nutmeg
1/4 teaspoon baking powder
1/2 cup butter
1/2 cup plus 3 tablespoons
  sugar

1 egg , separated
2/3 cup milk
3 tablespoons melted butter
1 tablespoon cinnamon

Heat oven to 400°. Mix flour, baking soda, baking powder and nutmeg in a large bowl. Stir well. Cream butter and sugar until pale and fluffy. Add egg yolk and milk. Fold in well-beaten egg white. Mix together wet and dry ingredients. Spoon into greased muffin tins. Bake 20 minutes. Roll in melted butter, sugar and cinnamon.

Yield: 12 muffins.

HONEY BUNNIES

4 1/2 to 5 cups flour,
  divided
2 packages active dry yeast
1 teaspoon salt
2/3 cup evaporated milk
1/2 cup water

1/2 cup honey
1/2 cup butter, cut into pieces
2 eggs, beaten
Honey Glaze (recipe follows)
raisins

Combine 1 1/2 cups flour, undissolved yeast and salt in large bowl. Heat evaporated milk, water, honey and butter until warm. Gradually add to flour mixture; beat two minutes at medium speed of electric mixer, scraping bowl occasionally. Add eggs and 1/2 cup flour; beat two minutes at high speed. With spoon, stir in enough remaining flour to make soft dough. Place in greased bowl. Grease top; cover tightly with plastic wrap; refrigerate for two to 24 hours. Remove dough from refrigerator, punch down. Remove to floured surface. Divide dough into 15 equal pieces. Roll each into 20-inch rope. Divide each rope into one 12-inch; one five-inch; and three one-inch strips. Coil 12-inch strip to make body; coil five inch strip to make head. Attach head to body; pinch to seal. Shape remaining three strips into ears and tail and attach to body and head. Place on two large greased baking sheets. Cover; let rise in warm place until doubled in size, about 20 to 40 minutes. Bake at 375° for 12 to 15 minutes. Remove from sheets to wire racks. Brush with Honey Glaze while warm. Insert raisins for eyes. If desired, brush again with glaze before serving.

Honey Glaze
1/2 cup honey   1/4 cup butter

Combine honey and butter in small saucepan. Cook over low heat until butter melts, stirring occasionally.

Honey bunnies would be a wonderful project to make with your children, especially around Easter.

Yield: 15 bunnies.

ILK TOAST

1 piece of thick white bread	brown sugar
butter	1/2 cup milk
cinnamon	

Toast bread on both sides. Butter it and top it with cinnamon and granulated brown sugar. Place the toast in a soup dish, sugar side up. Heat one-half cup milk thoroughly but don't let it boil. Pour at once over the toast. Cut into small pieces.

Whenever a member of the nursery set is not feeling quite his jolly self, serve him milk toast for a comforting supper.

Serves: one.

NURSERY FINGERS

white bread slices   butter

Toast bread on both sides and butter. Then top with the one of the following.

Cinnamon Toast Fingers
1 tablespoon sugar   1 teaspoon cinnamon

Spread a combination sugar and cinnamon over one side of toast. Place under broiler until toasted. Cut into thin slices or child-size fingers.

Orange Sugar Fingers
4 tablespoons confectioner's   1 teaspoon orange juice
  sugar
1 teaspoon grated orange rind

Combine, orange rind and orange juice. Spread on one side of toast. Place under broiler until hot. Cut into fingers.

Wonderful nursery fingers of flavored toast go delightfully with weak tea.

$\mathcal{S}$OFT PRETZELS

1 package dry yeast	1 1/2 teaspoons sugar
1 1/2 cups warm water	2 eggs, beaten
(105°-115°)	kosher or sea salt
4 cups flour	

Dissolve yeast in water. Combine, flour, sugar and salt and add to yeast mixture. Mix well until blended. Turn onto floured surface and knead about five to ten minutes. Place in greased bowl and turn to grease top. Cover and let rise in warm place, free from draft, until doubled in bulk - about one hour. Heat oven to 475°. Punch down dough. Shape pretzels (see below for directions) and place on cookie sheet lined with aluminum foil. Brush egg on each pretzel and sprinkle with salt. Bake 12-15 minutes or until golden brown. Place on wire racks to cool. Eat warm from oven or dip in mustard.

How to roll
Break off a piece of dough the size of a golf ball (one and one-half inches). Keep remainder of dough covered when not being used. Roll into a "rope" about 15-inches long. Make a loop by carefully picking up the ends. Bring the left end of the loop over to the right end under the left. A twist will be formed in the center. For the traditional three hole shape, bring the ends over and down and press them against the sides of the loop.

Yield: 30 6-inch pretzels

The first pretzels were made by the monks at the Vatican in the fifth century and given out to the poor. If you stare at a pretzel and use plenty of imagination, you may be able to see the shape of a person with his arms folded, praying.

Salads & Dressings

Preceding Page: Salad from Off to the Zoo Picnic
For Menu: See Page 236

Jacksonville is a city of bridges. One of our newest additions, the Dames Point Bridge, officially named after Napolean Bonaparte Broward, offers spectacular views of the region and is a beautiful subject for bridge enthusiasts.

St. John's River, showing Draw Bridge,
Jacksonville, Fla.

When construction of the St. Johns River draw bridge was completed, the golden age of resort town Jacksonville came to an end. As the railway expanded, cities farther south along its line began to prosper form the tourist industry.

Photograph is from collections at The Jacksonville Historical Society Archives.

ℱORT CAROLINE GREEN BEAN SALAD

1 pound fresh green beans,
  left whole with ends
  trimmed
1 small onion (2 inches in
  diameter), finely minced
1 clove garlic, finely minced
1 cup salad tomatoes, halved

1 tablespoon dried Italian
  parsley
1 cup pitted whole ripe
  olives
1/2 cup grated Parmesan
  cheese
dressing (recipe follows)

Cook beans in boiling salted water until just tender. Drain
and let cool. Combine beans with onion, garlic, tomatoes,
parsley and ripe olives in large bowl. Add dressing and toss
well. Sprinkle with Parmesan cheese.

Dressing

6 tablespoons extra virgin
  olive oil
3 teaspoons Dijon mustard

2 tablespoons white wine
  vinegar
1 teaspoon fresh grated
  black pepper

Combine all ingredients and add to salad.
Serves: six.

𝒜VONDALE BROCCOLI SALAD

2 bunches fresh broccoli
  flowerets
1 medium red onion (3 inches
  in diameter), chopped

1/2 jar real bacon bits
1 cup raisins
1 6-ounce can mushrooms
dressing (recipe follows)

Toss together the broccoli, onion, bacon, raisins and mushrooms in a large bowl. Add the dressing 30 minutes prior to
serving and marinate in the refrigerator.

Dressing

1 cup mayonnaise-based
  salad dressing

2 teaspoons sugar
1 tablespoon white wine
  vinegar

Combine the ingredients and blend until smooth.
Serves: 8 to 10.

ZESTY THREE BEAN SALAD

2 medium limes
3/4 cup thick and chunky
salsa (1/2 of 12-ounce jar)
1/4 cup salad oil
1 1/2 teaspoons chili
powder
1 teaspoon salt
1 15- to 16-ounce can black
beans, drained

1 15- to 19-ounce can garbanzo beans, drained
1 15 1/4- to 19-ounce can red
kidney beans, drained
2 large celery stalks, thinly
sliced
1 small red onion (2 inches in
diameter), thinly sliced
1 medium size tomato, diced

Squeeze juice from limes. Stir in salsa, salad oil, chili powder
and salt in a large bowl. Add beans, celery, onion and tomato.
Toss to mix well. Allow flavors to blend at least 30 minutes.
Serve the salad at room temperature or refrigerate to serve
chilled.

Serves: 10.

VEGGIE-CAULIFLOWER SALAD

1 small head of cauliflower
3/4 pound mushrooms
4 stalks of celery
1 large green pepper
4 radishes
1 English cucumber, unpeeled

1 tablespoon chopped
parsley
salt and ground pepper to
taste
dressing (recipe follows)

Thinly slice all the vegetables. Mix well. Cover and refrigerate. Add the dressing to the salad when ready to serve.

Dressing
1/4 cup white wine vinegar   1/2 cup extra virgin olive
oil

Whisk the vinegar and olive oil to blend.

Serves: four.

$\mathscr{S}$WEET AND SOUR CHINESE CABBAGE SLAW

1/2 medium head cabbage, finely shredded
1 medium carrot, shredded
4 green onions, finely chopped including green tops

1/2 cup raisins
2 tablespoons sesame seeds
1/4 cup slivered almonds
dressing (recipe follows)

Roast the sesame seeds and almonds in skillet until golden brown. Set aside. Toss the cabbage, green onions and raisins together. Add the almonds and the sesame seeds. Add the dressing and toss well. Refrigerate for at least two hours before serving.

Dressing
2 teaspoons soy sauce
2 tablespoons white wine vinegar
2 tablespoons sugar

3 tablespoons salad oil
1 tablespoon sesame oil (optional)
2 tablespoons water

Combine the dressing ingredients in a sauce pan. Bring to a boil. Combine the hot dressing with salad.

Serves: four.

These wild ponies from Ft. George Island provided children with hours of pleasure.

$\mathcal{B}$ROCCOLI AND CHICKEN SALAD ST. NICHOLAS

2 heads broccoli
2 tablespoons peanut oil
2 to 3 chicken breasts
1 cup parsley, chopped

4 green onions
cottage cheese and dill
   dressing (recipe follows)

Clean the broccoli. Trim off the toughest parts of the stems and cut the upper parts of the steams and the tops into small pieces or flowerets. Blanch in boiling water with the peanut oil. Simmer for about five minutes, then drain and plunge into cold water. Chill. Cook the chicken by roasting or poaching. Debone, cut up and chill. Combine the broccoli, chicken, parsley and onions in a large bowl. Toss with the dressing.

Cottage Cheese and Dill
  Dressing
1/2 cup cottage cheese
1/2 cup mayonnaise
1/2 cup milk
1 tablespoon olive oil
2 tablespoons wine vinegar
  or lemon juice

1/8 teaspoon sugar
salt and pepper to taste
1 clove garlic, crushed
1 teaspoon dried dill weed

Blend the ingredients. Refrigerate for a day before serving. Makes one and three-quarters cups of dressing.

Serves: four as a main dish.

$\mathcal{C}$HUTNEY CHICKEN SALAD

6 chicken breasts, cooked,
  deboned and cut up
1 1/2 cups sliced celery
1 bunch green onions, sliced

2 8-ounce cans pineapple
  chunks, reserve juice
1 1/2 cups cashews
dressing (recipe follows)

Combine chicken, celery, green onions, pineapple and cashews in large bowl. Toss with the dressing and serve.

Dressing
reserved juice from pineapple
6 ounces sour cream
3/4 cup mayonnaise

1 1/2 teaspoon curry
  powder
1/3 to 1/2 of 12 1/2-ounce
  jar of chutney

Mix the dressing ingredients.

Serves: 8 to 12 as main dish.

*C*HINESE CHICKEN SALAD

2 cups chicken, cooked and
  cubed
1 head of lettuce
4 to 5 green onions, chopped

2 tablespoons sesame seeds,
  roasted
1 package wonton skins
dressing (recipe follows)

Clean lettuce. Tear into a large salad bowl. Add the onions
and chicken. Cover with a paper towel and place in refrigerator. Lightly brown the wonton skins in hot oil on both sides.
Drain on paper towel. Before serving, add sesame seeds and
broken wontons to the salad. Pour on dressing and toss.

Dressing
4 tablespoons sugar

6 tablespoons rice vinegar
1/2 cup oil

Combine the dressing ingredients in a container with a tight
fitting lid and shake well.

Serves: six to eight.

*H*ONEY MUSTARD TURKEY SALAD

2 cups chopped cooked
  turkey
6 slices bacon, cooked and
  crumbled
1/4 cup thin strips of sweet
  red pepper
1/4 cup sliced green onions
1 2-ounce package roasted
  cashews

lettuce leaves
sweet red pepper rings, to
  garnish
Chow Mein noodles, to garnish
dressing (recipe follows)

Combine turkey, bacon, red pepper strips and onion in a large bowl and set aside. Toss with dressing. Cover and refrigerate. Stir in the cashews just before serving. Present on lettuce leaves and pepper rings. Sprinkle with Chow Mein noodles.

Dressing
1/2 cup mayonnaise
2 tablespoons Dijon mustard

3/4 teaspoon soy sauce
3/4 teaspoon lemon juice

Mix ingredients together and toss with salad.

Serves: four as a main dish.

*P*ENSACOLA PASTA SALAD

1 box small shell-shaped
  pasta
1 pound shrimp (cooked and
  deveined) or 1 cup ham
  chunks
1/2 cup cubed tomato
1/4 cup diced celery

1/4 cup black or green
  olives, sliced
1 tablespoon garlic salt
1 cup broccoli
1 cup grated Cheddar
  cheese
3 tablespoon Italian
  dressing

Cook pasta according to package directions. Drain and let cool. Cut broccoli into small pieces. Microwave the broccoli for 50 seconds, if desired. Mix all the ingredients with dressing and serve.

Two tablespoons of Parmesan cheese and two tablespoons of mayonnaise or melted butter may be used instead of the Italian dressing.

Serves: 8 to 10.

VENETIAN PASTA SALAD

2 cups orzo (rice shaped
    pasta)
2 chicken bouillon cubes
2 tablespoons salad oil
3 small zucchini (8 ounces,
    each), diced
1 medium onion (3 inches in
    diameter), diced
1 medium green pepper, cut
    into thin strips

1/2 teaspoon salt
1 5 3/4-ounce can pitted ripe
    olive, drained and sliced
1 4-ounce can whole pimentos, drained and cut into
    thin strips
dressing (recipe follows)

Prepare the orzo as the package directs but add the bouillon. Drain orzo and place in a large bowl. Set aside. Cook zucchini, onion and green pepper in salad oil over medium heat in a large skillet until vegetables are tender and crisp. Sprinkle with salt. Combine the cooked vegetables with the orzo. Add the olives and pimentos. Toss with the dressing. Cover and refrigerate one hour to blend flavors. Stir occasionally.

Dressing
3 tablespoons white wine
    vinegar
2 teaspoons dry mustard

1/4 teaspoon sugar
1 1/2 teaspoons salt

Combine the dressing ingredients.

Serves: eight.

$\mathcal{L}$UXEMBOURG SALAD

12 slices thick bacon, cut into
  1-inch pieces
4 slices day-old bread, cut
  into 1-inch squares
Luxembourg Dressing
  (recipe follows)

9 cups salad greens
  (spinach and Romaine
  lettuce) torn
1 1/2 cups blue cheese,
  crumbled

Fry the bacon pieces in a medium sized skillet until crisp. Drain on paper towels and reserve the fat in skillet. Slowly saute´ the bread in hot bacon fat until crisp and brown. Prepare the salad dressing. Combine the salad greens, bacon, croutons and blue cheese in a salad bowl. Add dressing, toss and serve immediately.

Luxembourg Dressing

4 cloves garlic, finely minced
1/3 cup balsamic vinegar
2 tablespoons fresh lemon
  juice
1 1/2 tablespoons Dijon
  mustard

1 1/2 tablespoons mixed salad
  herbs (parsley, chives,
  chervil and tarragon)
1 cup olive oil
salt and freshly ground pepper, to taste

Whisk the garlic, vinegar, lemon juice and mustard together in a mixing bowl. Whisk in the herbs. Gradually whisk in the oil. Season to taste with salt and pepper.

Serves: 8 to 10.

$\mathcal{S}$WISS AND SESAME SALAD

1 large head of Romaine
  lettuce
6 green onions, thinly sliced
  including tops

1 cup grated Swiss cheese
1/2 cup sesame seeds,
  toasted
Vinaigrette (recipe follows)

Tear the lettuce into bite size pieces and add the onions. Add the cheese and sesame seeds and toss. Toss with vinaigrette immediately before serving.

Vinaigrette
1/3 cup red wine vinegar

2/3 cup vegetable oil
1 tablespoon Greek seasoning

Shake all ingredients together in jar and refrigerate.

Serves: four to six.

$\mathcal{A}$LMOND MANDARIN ORANGE SALAD

3 tablespoons sugar
1/2 cup sliced almonds
dressing (recipe follows
1/2 head iceberg or Bibb
  lettuce

1/2 head Romaine lettuce
3 green onions, sliced
1 cup chopped celery
1 11-ounce can mandarin
  oranges, drained

Cook sugar and almonds over medium heat. Stir constantly until the sugar is dissolved and almonds are coated. Be careful, they burn easily! Cool the almonds and store in an airtight container. Prepare the dressing. Toss the lettuces with onions and celery. Add the almonds and oranges immediately before serving. Toss the salad with dressing.

Dressing
1/4 cup canola oil
2 tablespoons vinegar
2 tablespoons sugar
dash pepper

1 tablespoon parsley,
  chopped
dash hot pepper sauce
1/2 teaspoon salt

Mix all dressing ingredients by shaking in a jar and chill

Serves: four to six.

GREENS WITH PEARS AND ROQUEFORT

Dressing (recipe follows)
12 ounces watercress, tough stems removed
7 ounces frisce lettuce or curly endive or leaf lettuce

2 pears, cored and slivered
1 pound roasted chestnuts or water chestnuts, sliced
4 ounces Roquefort cheese, crumbled

Prepare the dressing. Wash the greens, dry and place in bowl. Add the chestnuts and pears. Toss with the dressing. Arrange on plates and top with the cheese.

Dressing
1/2 cup red wine vinegar
1 cup virgin olive oil
1 1/2 teaspoons salt

1 1/2 teaspoons chopped shallots
1/2 teaspoon freshly ground pepper

In a bowl, whisk dressing ingredients to blend.

Serves: 12.

GARLICKY GREEN SALAD

1 14-ounce can artichoke hearts, drained and quartered
1 14-ounce can heart of palm, drained and slices
3 cups tightly packed, torn Boston lettuce
2 cups tightly packed, torn fresh spinach

1 cup tightly packed, torn fresh watercress
1 tablespoon fresh chives, chopped
dressing (recipe follows)
tomato wedges for garnish

Combine the artichoke hearts, heart of palm, lettuce, spinach, watercress and chives in a large bowl. Pour the dressing over salad and toss well. Garnish with tomato wedges and serve.

Dressing

1 cup nonfat or low fat buttermilk
2 tablespoons minced parsley
2 tablespoons reduced fat
mayonnaise
2 tablespoons extra virgin
olive oil

2 tablespoons white wine
vinegar
3 cloves garlic, minced
1/4 teaspoon salt
1 1/2 teaspoons coarsely
ground black pepper

Combine the dressing ingredients in jar. Cover tightly and
shake. Refrigerate.

Serves: 12.

DEERWOOD SALAD WITH PARMESAN DRESSING

1/2 head iceberg lettuce,
chopped in bite size pieces
1 small head Romaine lettuce,
chopped into bite size pieces
1/4 pound Italian salami,
finely diced

1/4 pound Mozzarella
cheese, finely chopped
1 cup canned garbanzo
beans or chick peas,
drained and rinsed
dressing (recipe follows)

Combine the salad ingredients in a glass bowl. Chill while
preparing dressing. Pour the dressing over the salad just
before serving and toss lightly.

Dressing

5 tablespoons vegetable oil
2 tablespoons white wine or
white vinegar
1 teaspoon dry mustard

1 teaspoon salt, optional
1/2 teaspoon black pepper
1/2 cup grated Parmesan
cheese

Combine the dressing ingredients in a jar with a tight-fitting
lid. Shake well.

Serves: six to eight.

ORTEGA COMPANY SALAD
With Raspberry Vinaigrette

1 head Bibb lettuce, torn into bite size pieces
1/2 pound fresh spinach, torn into bite size pieces
2 oranges, peeled and sectioned
2 Red Delicious apples, unpeeled and thinly sliced
1 kiwi fruit, thinly sliced
1/2 cup coarsely chopped walnuts, toasted
Raspberry Vinaigrette (recipe follows)

Combine lettuce, spinach, oranges, apples, kiwi and walnuts in a large bowl. Toss with the dressing.

Raspberry Vinaigrette
1/2 cup vegetable oil
1/4 cup raspberry vinegar
1 tablespoon honey
1/2 teaspoon grated orange rind
1/4 teaspoon salt
1/8 teaspoon pepper

Combine all ingredients in a jar; cover tightly. Shake vigorously and chill.

Serves: eight.

CAESAR RICE SALAD

1 1/2 cups regular long grain rice
3 large tomatoes
3/4 cup finely chopped parsley
2 tablespoons salad oil
1 1/2 teaspoons salt
1 1/2 teaspoons cracked black pepper

Prepare rice as the label directions suggest. Mince the tomato. When the rice is done, add the tomato and remaining ingredients. Toss gently. Cover and refrigerate until cool minimum one hour.

Serves: eight.

NEPTUNE BEACH SHRIMP MOLD

1 envelope unflavored gelatin
1 can tomato soup
1/2 cup boiling water
1 8-ounce package cream
  cheese
1 cup mayonnaise
1 pound of cooked shrimp,
  diced
1 cup diced celery
1/4 cup minced onion

Combine the gelatin, soup and water. Stir until the gelatin dissolves. Put this mixture into a blender with the cream cheese and mayonnaise. Blend until smooth. Add the shrimp, celery and onion. Pour into a large mold. Chill until it sets. Unmold and decorate plate with greens. Serve with crackers.

Serves: 12.

CANNELLINI BEAN AND TUNA SALAD

1 6 1/8-ounce can albacore
  solid white water packed
  tuna, drained
dressing (recipe follows)
1 16-ounce can cannellini
  beans (white kidney
  beans), drained and well
  rinsed
1/4 cup finely chopped
  white onion
1 cup chopped fresh tomato
1 clove garlic, finely
  chopped
2 tablespoons fresh basil or
  1 tablespoon dried basil

Drain the tuna and break into chunks. Prepare the dressing. Combine the beans, tuna, onion, tomatoes, garlic and basil. Add the dressing and toss well. Chill and serve on lettuce leaves.

Dressing
2 tablespoons red wine
  vinegar
4 tablespoons olive oil
dash of black pepper

Whisk the dressing ingredients together to blend.

Serves: six.

CURRIED SHRIMP SALAD MAYPORT
With Papaya

1 pound large shrimp, peeled, deveined and cooked
1 pound sea scallops, halved if large
dressing (recipe follows)

4 teaspoons fresh parsley
4 cups tender lettuce
4 cups spinach
2 papaya or 4 nectarines, peeled and seeded

Chill the shrimp. Broil the scallops until they are opaque and chill. Prepare the dressing and stir in the shrimp, scallops and parsley. Arrange a bed of lettuce in the center of a plate for each serving. Surround with the spinach. Mound the salad on top of the greens. Cut the papaya or nectarines into long slivers. Arrange the slivers in a swirl on top of each salad.

Dressing
1 cup nonfat plain yogurt
1/2 teaspoon cardamon
1/2 teaspoon cumin

1/4 teaspoon coriander
2 tablespoons honey, or to taste
1/4 teaspoon cinnamon

Combine the dressing ingredients and refrigerate. Whisk to blend if it separates.

Serves: four as main dish.

ENGLISH CUCUMBER AND POTATO SALAD

4 medium red potatoes, boiled, peeled and thinly sliced
2 medium English cucumbers, unpeeled and thinly sliced

1 medium (3 inches in diameter) sweet onion, sliced in very thin rings
dressing (recipe follows)

Drain the potatoes on a paper towel for at least one hour. Mix the vegetables with the dressing and chill.

Dressing
1 cup light mayonnaise
1 cup sour cream or plain
  yogurt
1 tablespoon dried dill weed

2 teaspoons salt
3 to 4 tablespoons white
  wine vinegar
dash Worcestershire sauce

Combine the dressing ingredients and pour over the salad.

Serves: four.

HEART OF PALM SALAD

Dressing (recipe follows)
1 14-ounce can hearts of
  palm, drained and cut
  into 1/2 inch pieces

6 cups torn Romaine lettuce
  (1 large head)

Prepare the dressing and chill at least eight hours. Prior to serving, arrange the hearts of palm on bed of lettuce on individual serving plates. Top with dressing.

Dressing
1 cup olive oil
1/2 cup white vinegar
1/2 cup finely chopped
  celery
1/4 cup finely chopped
  sweet red pepper

1/4 cup finely chopped onion
1/4 cup finely chopped dill
  pickle
6 ripe olives, finely chopped
2 cloves garlic, crushed
1/4 teaspoon capers

Combine the dressing ingredients and chill at least eight hours for flavors to blend.

Serves: six.

*F*IESTA SALAD TOSS

dressing (recipe follows)
4 cups lettuce, shredded
1 1/2 cups jicama, peeled
and cut into strips
1 cup cucumber, peeled and
cut into strips
1 cup tomato wedges

1 4-ounce can sliced green
chilies
1 1/2 cups cheddar cheese,
cubed
2 cups tortilla chips, half
coarsely crushed
1 avocado, sliced

Prepare the dressing. Line the salad bowl with lettuce and fill the center with jicama, cucumber, tomato, chilies and cheese. Chill. Just before serving, toss the salad with crushed chips and one cup or more of the dressing. Garnish with the whole chips and avocado.

Dressing

1 envelope ranch style
dressing mix
1 tablespoon lime juice

1 teaspoon chili powder
2 cups sour cream
1/2 teaspoon cumin

Whisk together the dressing ingredients. Chill.

Serves: four to six.

*B*ABY SQUASH AND MUSHROOM STIR-FRY SALAD

2 tablespoons salad oil
1 pound miniature zucchini,
yellow straight neck
squash and pattypan
squash (about 40 miniature
squash) or 1 6-ounce zuc-
chini, 1 6-ounce yellow
straight neck squash and 2
3-ounce pattypan squashes

1/2 pound medium size
mushrooms
3/4 teaspoon salt
1/8 teaspoon crushed red
pepper (optional)
1 tablespoon soy sauce
fresh rosemary

Heat salad oil in a 12-inch skillet over medium heat until hot. If using the larger squashes, cut into bite size pieces. Cook the squash, mushrooms, salt and crushed pepper until the vegetables are tender about 10 minutes. Stir occasionally. Stir in the soy sauce. Add rosemary leaves to taste. Serve warm or cover and refrigerate to serve cold later. Garnish with a sprig of rosemary prior to serving.

Serves: four.

*B*AYMEADOWS VEGGIE SALAD

1 16-ounce can French cut
  green beans, drained
1 8-ounce can young peas,
  drained
1 10-ounce can white corn,
  drained

1 cup chopped celery
1 cup chopped green pepper
1/2 cup chopped scallions
1 2-ounce jar chopped
  pimentos
dressing (recipe follows)

Combine the vegetables in a large glass bowl. Pour the dressing over the vegetables and mix thoroughly. Refrigerate in a covered container for 24 hours.

Dressing
1/4 cup vegetable oil

3/4 cup vinegar
1/2 cup sugar

Mix together and let stand until the sugar dissolves. Stir and pour over the vegetables.

Serves: six to eight.

TOMATO AND ONION SALAD

3 large ripe tomatoes, cut
  crosswise into 6 slices each
1 large red onion, peeled and
  thinly sliced crosswise
salt, to taste

freshly ground pepper to
  taste
3 tablespoons chopped
  fresh basil leaves
dressing (recipe follows)

Arrange the tomato and onion slices on a serving platter.
Place one onion slice between every two tomato slices.
Sprinkle the tomatoes with salt and pepper, if desired. Pour
the dressing over the tomatoes and onion. Sprinkle the salad
with the basil and serve.

<u>Dressing</u>
3 tablespoons red wine
  vinegar

3 tablespoons olive oil
3 tablespoons grated
  Parmesan cheese

Combine the dressing ingredients in a small bowl or jar.
Blend well.

Serves: four to six.

RIBAULT RADISH AND CARROT SALAD

1 cup chopped radishes
2 cups shredded carrots
1 cup sliced green onions,
  including tops

dressing (recipe follows)
lettuce leaves to garnish

Combine the vegetables. Toss with the dressing until well
blended. Chill and serve on lettuce leaves.

<u>Dressing</u>
1 tablespoon Dijon mustard
1 tablespoon white wine
  vinegar

2 tablespoons olive or vegetable oil
freshly ground pepper to taste

Whisk the dressing ingredients until well blended.

Serves: six

*F*ATOOSH SALAD

2 loaves Syrian bread
1 bunch green onions, finely
chopped
2 cucumbers, peeled and
chopped
2 bunches parsley, cleaned
and finely chopped

2 bunches green mint,
finely chopped
8 medium tomatoes (3
inches in diameter), cut
into small wedges
dressing (recipe follows)

Toast the Syrian bread and break into small pieces. Set aside
to cool. Prepare the dressing. Combine the vegetables and
add dressing. Add the bread and toss lightly.

Dressing
1 cup olive oil
juice of 5 lemons

3 cloves garlic, mashed
salt and pepper to taste

Combine the oil, lemon juice, garlic and spices. Blend well.

Serves: eight.

*D*ELICIOUS CABBAGE SALAD

1/2 head cabbage, finely
chopped
2 teaspoons sesame seeds,
toasted
1/2 cup slivered almonds,
toasted

4 green onions, chopped
1 3.1 ounce package Chi-
nese Ramon chicken
flavor noodles
dressing (recipe follows)

Mix all ingredients. Prepare the dressing and pour on the
salad right before serving.

Dressing
2 teaspoons sugar
1 tablespoon vinegar
1/2 cup vegetable oil

1 teaspoon salt
1/4 teaspoon pepper
seasoning pack from
noodles

Mix the dressing ingredients together until well blended.

Serves: six

$\mathcal{S}$UPERB TORTELLINI CHICKEN SALAD

8 chicken breast halves
enough cold water to cover
  chicken
2 tablespoons olive oil
2 garlic cloves, minced
9 ounces fresh tortellini
  pasta
1 medium green pepper,
  seeded and chopped
3 stalks celery, thinly sliced

1 medium purple onion,
  chopped
1/4 pound smoked Gruyére
  cheese, cut into 1/2 inch
  cubes
1/2 teaspoon salt
freshly ground pepper, to
  taste
Vinaigrette (recipe follows)

Place the chicken breasts in a large pot and barely cover with the cold water. Bring the water to a boil over high heat. Turn down the heat and simmer the chicken for 15 minutes or until barely cooked through. Let the chicken cool slightly in the liquid. When the chicken can be handled, remove the meat from the bones and cut into one-half by three inch strips. Heat the olive oil in a large skillet, add the garlic and sauté until golden brown. Remove the garlic and reserve. Add the chicken to the skillet and sauté for one minute, stirring constantly. Cook the tortellini according to package directions. Drain and rinse quickly in cold water. Place the chicken, reserved garlic, tortellini, green pepper, celery, onion, cheese, salt and pepper in a large, three quart bowl and toss together. Prepare the vinaigrette and pour over the salad. Chill in the refrigerator several hours before serving.

<u>Vinaigrette</u>
3/4 cup cider vinegar
1/4 cup honey

2 tablespoons Dijon mustard
1 teaspoon dry mustard
3/4 cup corn oil

Prepare the vinaigrette in a blender. Place the vinegar, honey and mustards in the blender and blend. While the blender is running, slowly drizzle in the oil. Blend until creamy.

It tastes even better the second day.

Serves: eight.

NEW WAVE SALAD

2 cups fresh basil
1 tablespoon olive oil
8 ounces fettucine
1 1/2 cup red wine basil
  vinaigrette (recipe follows)
1 pound tender green beans
6 ripe plum tomatoes, cut into
  8 pieces

2 cups black olives
2 tablespoons chopped
  fresh parsley
4 ounces Parmesan cheese,
  not grated

Arrange the basil leaves in small stacks. Slice diagonally into slivers, reserve one-half cup for vinaigrette. Bring a large pot of water to boil. Add the oil and fettucine. Cook at rolling boil until just tender. Drain and rinse with cold water. Place the fettucine in a large mixing bowl. Add one-half cup vinaigrette and toss, set aside. Bring a pot of water to boil. Add the green beans and simmer until just tender, five to eight minutes. Drain and rinse under cold water and set aside. Place the pasta in a serving bowl. Layer with the tomatoes, then beans, olives and one-half cup basil. Sprinkle with parsley and pour remaining vinaigrette over the salad. Scrape the Parmesan cheese with a vegetable peeler to make thin wide shavings. Place on top of the salad. Toss well before serving.

Serves: six.

RED WINE BASIL VINAIGRETTE

2 cloves garlic, crushed
2 tablespoons Dijon mustard
1/2 cup red wine vinegar
1 teaspoon fresh ground
  pepper

1 cup extra virgin olive oil
1/2 cup fresh basil, slivered
  as prepared in recipe above
1/2 cup chopped fresh
  parsley

Combine the garlic, mustard, vinegar and pepper in a small bowl. Whisk well, add the oil in a small stream. Whisk constantly until the vinaigrette has thickened slightly. Fold in the basil and parsley.

CHICORY-ORANGE SALAD
With Watercress Dressing

3 heads chicory, washed   Dressing (recipe follows)
2 oranges, peeled

Cut the chicory into small pieces. Slice the oranges thinly across sections, then cut into half circle slices. Mix chicory and oranges in a salad bowl. Prepare the dressing and pour over the salad. Serve.

Dressing

2 bunches watercress,
  chopped
2 tablespoons low fat yogurt

1 teaspoon Dijon mustard
3 tablespoon tarragon or
  white vinegar
salt and pepper to taste

Combine the vinegar, mustard, pepper, salt and watercress. Add this mixture to the yogurt to make the dressing.

Serves: six.

ATLANTIC BEACH TUNA SALAD

1 6-ounce can tuna packed
  in water
1/2 cup low fat yogurt
1/2 cup chopped celery

1 small onion, (2 inches in
  diameter,) chopped
1 teaspoon lemon juice
1/2 teaspoon Dijon mustard

Drain the tuna. Combine tuna with yogurt and other ingredients. Garnish as desired.

Serves: four.

SPINACH SALAD WITH ROSEWOOD
STRAWBERRY DRESSING

1/2 pound spinach leaves
1 red onion, thinly sliced
  crosswise
20 large strawberries

1 11-ounce can mandarin
  oranges, drained
Rosewood Strawberry
  Dressing (recipe follows)

Wash the spinach in lots of cold water to remove any grit. Remove thick stems and pat the leaves dry. Separate the onion slices into individual rings. Toss together the spinach, onions, strawberries and oranges. Serve with dressing drizzled on it.

<u>Rosewood Strawberry</u>
<u>Dressing</u>
1/2 cup low fat yogurt
1/3 cup chopped red onions
1/4 cup sliced strawberries
3 tablespoons lemon juice

2 teaspoons tarragon vinegar
1 teaspoon honey
1 teaspoon paprika
1/2 teaspoon grated lemon
  rind
dash of dry mustard

Place all the ingredients in a blender. Process on medium speed until smooth. Store tightly covered in the refrigerator. Will keep for three to five days. Stir before serving.

Serves: eight.

Mrs. Buckland, Riverside Avenue, ca. 1905.
Photograph is from collections at The Riverside/Avondale Preservation Archives.

MARINATED VEGETABLE SALAD

2 cups cauliflower florets,
  broken into bite size pieces
2 cups broccoli florets, broken
  into bite size pieces
1 cup thinly sliced carrots
1 cup 1-inch green bean pieces
Dressing (recipe follows)

2 small yellow squash cut
  into 1/4-inch slices,
  about 2 cups
2 small zucchini cut into
  1/4-inch slices, about 2
  cups

Combine the cauliflower, broccoli, carrots and green beans in
a steamer basket. Cook five minutes. Place in a colander and
rinse under cold water. Prepare the dressing. Combine the
steamed vegetables and squashes in a large bowl. Pour the
dressing over the vegetables and toss gently. Cover and
refrigerate for several hours before serving. Stir occasionally.

<u>Dressing</u>
2 tablespoons frozen apple
  juice concentrate
1/4 cup cider vinegar
1/4 cup lemon juice

1 tablespoon grated onion
1 teaspoon dry mustard
1 clove garlic, minced
1 teaspoon dried oregano
1/2 teaspoon anise seed

Combine the dressing ingredients in one quart screw top jar.
Shake well to blend.

Serves: six.

$\mathcal{B}$OK CHOY SALAD

6 cups torn bok choy
1/3 cup walnut halves

1/4 cup raisins
dressing (recipe follows)

Prepare the dressing. Toss the bok choy, walnuts and raisins with the dressing in a large bowl.

Dressing
1/4 cup salad oil
3 tablespoon lemon or lime juice
1 tablespoon honey
1 1/2 teaspoon soy sauce

1 teaspoon sesame seed, toasted
1/2 teaspoon paprika
1/2 teaspoon salt

Combine the dressing ingredients in a screw top jar. Shake well to blend.

Serves: six.

Doubin Holmes residence, Riverside and Fisk.
Photograph is from collections at The Riverside/Avondale Preservation Archives.

SAN JOSE PASTA

1 1/2 cups black beans or
    1 15-ounce can
1 10-ounce package frozen
    corn
1 1/4 cup prepared salsa

1 fresh tomato, chopped
1 8-ounce package small sea
    shell pasta, cooked and
    drained

Mix the black beans, corn and salsa in a saucepan. Heat slightly. Add the fresh tomatoes and pour over the pasta in a large bowl. Garnish with tortilla chips.

Serves: six to eight.

HAM AND LIMA BEAN SALAD

2 10-ounce packages frozen
    lima beans
2 cups sliced fresh
    mushrooms
1 cup chopped red onion
1/2 cup finely chopped fully
    cooked ham

1/3 cup chopped ripe olives
1/4 cup snipped parsley
1 4-ounce jar diced pimentos,
    drained
Dressing (recipe follows)

Cook the lima beans according to package directions. Drain. Rinse in cold water, drain again. Combine beans, mushrooms, onion, ham, olives, parsley and pimento in a large mixed bowl. Prepare the dressing. Pour the dressing over the bean mixture. Toss the bean mixture to coat. Cover and chill three to 24 hours before serving. Stir occasionally.

Dressing
1/3 cup tarragon or white
    wine vinegar
1/4 cup olive or salad oil
2 cloves garlic, minced

1/2 teaspoon sugar
1/2 teaspoon salt
1/2 teaspoon lemon juice
1/8 teaspoon pepper

Combine the dressing ingredients in a screw top jar. Cover and shake to combine.

Serves: 8 to 10.

$\mathscr{N}$O FAT DIJON DRESSING

3/4 cup water
1/4 cup balsamic vinegar
3 teaspoons capers
2 teaspoons Dijon mustard

1 1/2 teaspoons dried basil
1 tablespoon chopped
   fresh parsley

Combine all the ingredients. Store covered in refrigerator.

Yield: one and one-quarter cups.

$\mathscr{S}$AN JOSE POPPY SEED FRUIT DIP

2 cups sour cream
1/4 cup brown sugar

2 tablespoons Grenadine
1 tablespoon poppy seeds

Combine all ingredients. Serve with fresh fruit.

Yield: two and one-quarter cups.

$\mathscr{A}$MARETTO FRUIT DIP

1 7- to 8- ounce jar marshmallow cream
1 8-ounce package cream
  cheese

5 to 6 tablespoons Amaretto

Combine all ingredients until smooth. Serve this with
fresh fruit.

Yield: two and one-quarter cups.

RIVERSIDE MIX AND MATCH DRESSINGS

Classic Vinaigrette

2/3 cup olive or salad oil   1/4 teaspoon salt
1/3 cup wine vinegar   dash pepper

In a small bowl, mix all the ingredients.

Yield: one cup.

Creamy Dressing

1/2 cup mayonnaise   1/2 teaspoon sugar
2 tablespoons milk   1/4 teaspoon salt
1 tablespoon wine vinegar   dash pepper

In a small bowl, mix all ingredients.

Yield: three-quarters cup.

Start with the Classic Vinaigrette and Creamy Dressing and you can create 50 different dressings simply by adding one of the following ingredients!

1/2 cup crumbled blue cheese
2 teaspoons chopped parsley and 2 teaspoons chopped fresh
   tarragon or basil
1 tablespoon Dijon mustard
2 tablespoons sweet pickle relish or chopped dill pickle
1 tablespoon anchovy paste
2 tablespoons chopped capers
1 garlic clove, minced
1/4 cup pimento stuffed olives, chopped
1 tablespoon prepared white horseradish
1/4 cup bottled chili sauce or catsup
1 tablespoon minced green onion or chives
2 tablespoons grated Parmesan cheese
2 tablespoons chopped, marinated, dried tomatoes
1 tablespoon grated, peeled gingerroot
1/4 cup chopped, roasted sweet pepper or pimento
1/4 cup minced arugula
1 tablespoon chopped fresh dill, rosemary or basil
1 teaspoon chili powder

1/4 cup mild or hot salsa
2 tablespoons chopped sweet red onion
1/4 cup mashed avocado
1 hard cooked egg, finely chopped
1/2 cup shredded sharp Cheddar cheese
2 teaspoons crushed caraway seeds

CURRIED DRESSING

1/2 cup plus 2 tablespoons
  rice vinegar
2 tablespoons chutney,
  chopped in the blender
1/2 teaspoon salt
1/2 tablespoon curry powder

1/2 tablespoon dry
  mustard
4 drops hot pepper sauce
1/4 cup salad oil

Combine all the ingredients in a jar. Cover and shake to combine.

Yield: one cup.

WARM MUSTARD DRESSING

4 large eggs
4 tablespoons dry mustard
2/3 cup white vinegar
1 cup sugar

2 cups heavy cream,
  divided
1 teaspoon salt

Mix eggs, mustard, salt and sugar in food processor with steel blade. Add vinegar and one cup cream. Cook over very low heat in heavy saucepan. Stir constantly until thick, 15 to 20 minutes. Remove from heat and whisk in remaining one cup cream. May be stored in refrigerator for several weeks. Reheat before pouring over salad.

Great with all salads especially fresh spinach leaves with cut up apples, cocktail peanuts, shredded Parmesan cheese and shredded Romano cheese.

Yield: four cups.

HONEY JALAPENO DRESSING

1/4 teaspoon finely
   shredded lime peel
2 tablespoons lime juice
1 tablespoon honey
dash ground nutmeg

1/4 cup salad oil
1 to 2 teaspoons chopped
   fresh or canned jalapeno
   pepper

Combine all ingredients. Refrigerate. *Great over greens.*

Yield: one-third cup.

Ida Beerbower
Photograph is from collections at The Riverside/Avondale Preservation Archives.

Appetizers & Beverages

Preceding Page: Beverage from Poolside Party
For Menu: See Page 242

During the summer months, swimming pools become the social centers of family entertaining. This particular pool gracefully overlooks the St. Johns River.

The Dixieland Park was a major tourist attraction sporting a roller coaster and a carnival atmosphere. In the early 1900's, several film studios were located there.

Photograph is from collections at The Jacksonville Historical Society Archives.

*L*OWFAT CHILI AVOCADO DIP

2 ripe avocados, peeled,
  chopped and mashed
1 16 ounce can green beans,
  drained and chopped
1/4 cup lemon juice

2 teaspoons grated onion
1 teaspoon chili powder
1 teaspoon hot pepper
  sauce

Blend all ingredients. Cover and chill at least six hours.

Green beans are the secret in this reduced-fat version of guacamole.

Yield: three cups.

*R*EBECCA BATES BLUE CHEESE CAKE

1/3 cup fine bread crumbs
1/4 cup grated Parmesan
  cheese
3 1/2 (8 ounce) packages
  cream cheese, softened
4 large eggs
1/2 cup heavy cream
1/2 pound bacon

1 medium onion, finely
  chopped
1/2 pound crumbled blue
  cheese
salt and freshly ground
  pepper, to taste
2-3 drops hot pepper
  sauce

Heat oven to 300°. Sprinkle bread crumbs and Parmesan cheese in a buttered, watertight eight-inch round springform pan. Set aside. Combine cream cheese, eggs and cream in mixer. Saute´ bacon until crisp; drain and chop finely. Reserve one tablespoon drippings; saute onion in reserved tablespoon of drippings until clear. Add onions, bacon, blue cheese, salt, pepper and hot pepper sauce to cream cheese mixture. Pour into prepared springform pan. Set pan inside a larger one, pour boiling water two inches deep into larger pan. Bake one hour and 40 minutes. Turn off oven and let "cake" set for one hour. Remove pan from water. Cool two hours. Remove cake from springform pan and serve with crackers.

Yield: one eight-inch cake.

COWFORD COWBOY CAVIAR

1 can (15 ounces) black
   beans, rinsed and drained
1 4-ounce can chopped ripe
   olives, drained
1 small onion, finely
   chopped (1/4 cup)
1 clove of garlic, finely
   chopped
2 tablespoons oil
2 tablespoons lime juice

1/2 teaspoon salt
1/4 teaspoon crushed red
   pepper
1/4 teaspoon ground cumin
1/8 teaspoon pepper
8 ounces cream cheese,
   softened
2 hard-cooked eggs, peeled
   and chopped
1 green onion with top, sliced

Mix beans, olives, oil, lime juice, onion, garlic and spices.
Cover and refrigerate at least four hours. Spread cream
cheese in glass pie plate. Spoon bean mixture on top and
arrange eggs in circle on top of bean mixture at the edge of
plate. Sprinkle with green onion. Serve with crackers.

Serves: eight

CRAB AND CHEESE SPREAD

8 ounces cream cheese,
   softened
1 4 oz can white crabmeat
   (drained)
1 teaspoon horseradish
   sauce
1 tablespoon mayonnaise
1 tablespoon sour cream

3 finely chopped scallions
1 cup shredded Cheddar
   cheese
dash chili powder
dash garlic salt
splash hot pepper sauce
splash Worcestershire sauce
loaf round bread

Mix all ingredients, except bread, together. Chill at least four
hours. Scoop top out of bread, spoon mixture into bread and
serve with crackers or pita points.

Yield: two cups.

ARTICHOKE AND SHRIMP APPETIZER

1 large artichoke
3 cups water
3 tablespoons lemon juice
1 teaspoon butter or margarine
2 1/4 teaspoons finely
 chopped shallots
1/2 teaspoon minced garlic
1/2 (8-ounce) package light
 cream cheese, softened
1 tablespoon chopped green
 onions
1 tablespoon nonfat plain
 yogurt
1/2 teaspoon dried savory
1/8 teaspoon seasoned salt
1/8 teaspoon pepper
Dash of hot pepper sauce
30 large fresh shrimp,
 unpeeled
Garnishes: fresh parsley
 sprigs, pitted ripe olives,
 paprika

Wash artichoke by plunging up and down in cold water. Cut off stem end and trim about one-half inch from top. Remove loose bottom leaves. Place artichoke in a dutch oven, cover with water and add lemon juice. Bring to a boil. Cover, reduce heat and simmer 30 to 35 minutes or until lower leaves pull out easily. Drain and cool. Pull apart 30 leaves, and arrange on serving dish; set aside, reserving heart for another use. Bring three cups water to a boil; add shrimp, and cook three to five minutes or until shrimp turns pink. Drain and rinse with cold water. Peel and devein shrimp; refrigerate. Melt butter in a large skillet; add shallots and garlic. Cook over medium-high heat, stirring constantly, until tender. Stir in softened cream cheese, green onion, yogurt, savory, salt, pepper and hot sauce. Remove from heat. Cover and refrigerate. Spoon about one teaspoon cream cheese mixture onto each artichoke leaf just before serving; top with a shrimp. Garnish, if desired, and serve on a lettuce-lined tray.

Yield: 30 appetizers.

WARM BLUE CHEESE AND BACON DIP

7 bacon slices, diced
2 garlic cloves, minced
8 ounces cream cheese at
  room temperature
1/4 cup half and half
4 ounces crumbled blue
  cheese

2 tablespoons chopped fresh
  chives
3 tablespoons chopped
  smoked almonds (about one
  ounce)

Heat oven to 350°. Cook bacon in heavy, large skillet over medium high heat until almost crisp, about seven minutes. Drain excess fat from skillet. Add garlic and cook until bacon is crisp, about three minutes. Beat cream cheese with electric mixer until smooth. Add half and half and beat until combined. Stir in bacon mixture, blue cheese and chives. Transfer to two-cup oven proof baking dish. Cover with foil, bake until heated through about 30 minutes. Sprinkle with chopped almonds. Serve with crackers, bread and/or vegetables.

Yield: one and one-half cups

MONTEREY PEPPER CHEESE

1 very large, well shaped
  green bell pepper
4 tablespoons minced red
  bell pepper
8 ounces fat-free cream
  cheese

2 ounces diced extra sharp
  Cheddar cheese
2 teaspoons prepared mustard,
  mild or spicy
1-2 teaspoons chili powder

Slice off the top of the green pepper to form a cup. Remove seeds and membranes. Trim off top and discard stem. Combine cream cheese, Cheddar cheese, mustard and chilli powder in food processor, process until smooth. Fold in minced red pepper and spoon into pepper cup. Refrigerate until serving time. Serve with crackers, vegetables or pita chips.

Yield: one cup.

STUFFED CLAMS

6 1/2 oz chopped clams and liquid
1/2 cup finely chopped onion
1/2 cup finely chopped celery
1/4 cup finely chopped green or red bell pepper
4 tablespoons butter
2 tablespoons flour
2 tablespoons Parmesan cheese

salt and pepper to taste
dash Worcestershire sauce
sprinkle of oregano
12 crushed round buttery crackers
1 tablespoon butter melted and paprika
6-8 shallow baking shells

Heat oven to 350°. Sauté onion, celery and pepper until tender in four tablespoons butter. Add flour, cheese and seasonings. Add one-half cup crushed crackers. Stir in clams and liquid and cook over medium-low heat until bubbly. Divide among baking shells, sprinkle with remaining cracker crumbs and top with melted butter and paprika. Spoon mixture into shallow baking shells. Bake for 10-15 minutes.

Serves: six to eight.

DANA LEE'S SHRIMP SPREAD

1 7-ounce can shrimp, completely drained
1 12-ounce package cream cheese, softened
1 tablespoon horseradish

1 tablespoon grated onion
1 tablespoon lemon juice
2 dashes of hot pepper sauce, to taste
paprika to sprinkle over top

Mash shrimp and mix all ingredients together. Place in oven-proof dish and sprinkle with paprika. Bake at 375° for about 15 minutes. Serve warm, does not need to be kept over burner when served. Serve with party pumpernickel, melba toast or wheat crackers.

Yield: two cups.

*E*GGPLANT ANTIPASTO

3 cups peeled and cubed
  eggplant
1/3 cup green pepper,
  chopped
1 medium onion, chopped
3/4 cup sliced fresh mushrooms
2 garlic cloves, chopped
1/3 cup olive oil

1 cup tomato paste
2 teaspoons wine vinegar
1/2 cup green olives
1 1/2 teaspoon sugar
1 teaspoon oregano
1 teaspoon salt
1 teaspoon pepper
1/4 cup water

Place eggplant, green pepper, onion, mushrooms, garlic and oil in skillet. Cover and cook gently 10 minutes, over meduim heat, stirring occasionally. Add tomato paste, vinegar, olives, sugar, oregano, salt, pepper and water. Mix well, cover and simmer until eggplant is tender, about 30 minutes. Serve hot or cold as appetizer with melba rounds or pita points.

If served cold, spoon into hollowed purple cabbage, it's beautiful and tasty.

Yield: five to six cups.

*C*REAMY TOMATO SPREAD

8 ounces cream cheese,
  softened
1/2 cup sundried tomatoes,
  packed in oil

4 green onions

Place cream cheese, tomatoes and green onions in a food processor and process with on/off turns until smooth and well blended. Put in mold with plastic wrap over hanging edges so it can be easily removed. Chill four to six hours. Remove from mold and garnish with chopped parsley. Serve with crackers or crudites.

Yield: one cup.

$\mathcal{P}$ESTO BITES

Pesto
4 1/2 cups loosely packed
   fresh basil
1 cup extra virgin olive oil
1/2 cup pine nuts (optional)
5 cloves garlic
2 teaspoons salt
4 ounces freshly grated
   Parmesan cheese (1 cup)

Bites
2 French bread loaves, cut
   lengthwise
4 ounces cream cheese,
   softened
chopped sundried tomatoes,
   packed in oil

Heat oven to 450°. Puree basil, olive oil, pine nuts, garlic and salt in food processor until smooth. Stir in freshly grated Parmesan cheese and refrigerate to let flavors blend, approximately four hours. Top halved french bread with cream cheese, then pesto and sundried tomatoes. Bake for five minutes. Cut into wedges and serve warm.

Yield: 12 bites.

$\mathcal{B}$LACK BEAN DIP

1 16-ounce can black beans,
   rinsed and drained
1 tablespoon chopped red
   onion
2 tablespoons balsamic
   vinegar

1 tablespoon fresh orange
   juice
1 garlic clove, minced
salt and pepper to taste
5 whole wheat pita breads,
   split and cut into wedges

In blender or food processor combine beans, one-half tablespoon onion, vinegar, orange juice and garlic; blend until smooth. Season with salt and pepper and spoon into serving bowl. Garnish with remaining onion. Place pita wedges on baking sheet and broil until crisp and golden. Place dip on serving platter and surround with pita chips and vegetables.

Yield: two cups.

AVOCADO SALMON ROLLS

1/4 pound thin sliced
  smoked salmon
3 slices rye bread
1 tablespoon butter
lemon twists and dill sprigs,
  to garnish

Filling
1/4 cup cream cheese
1/2 avocado, mashed
1 small tomato, skinned,
  seeded and chopped
2 teaspoons chopped fresh dill
1/4 teaspoon ground black
  pepper

Place cheese for filling in bowl and beat until softened. Add avocado, stir until blended. Stir in tomato, dill and pepper. Place mixture into a pastry bag fitted with a one-half inch plain nozzle. Cut smoked salmon into 20 oblongs measuring one and one-half by one inch. Pipe a length of cheese mixture across top of short edge of salmon then roll-up neatly. Spread rye with butter, then cut into 20 rectangles to fit salmon rolls. Place a salmon roll on each piece. Garnish with lemon twists and dill sprigs.

Yield: 20.

BRIE EN CROÛTE

1/2 cup flour
dash of salt
1/4 cup butter, chilled and
  beaten

2 ounces cream cheese
1 wheel of Brie (14 ounce)
1 egg yolk
2 teaspoons water

Sift flour with the salt and cut in butter and the cream cheese to resemble coarse crumbs. Refrigerate overnight. Roll pastry out on a floured board to one-eighth inch thickness. Place the cheese in the middle and enclose with the pastry. Make a small hole in the middle to allow steam to escape. Refrigerate one hour. Heat oven to 450°. Mix egg yolk and water and brush the top of the pastry immediately before baking. Bake for 20 minutes.

Serves: six to eight.

$\mathscr{B}$RIE AND HERB CHEESE IN PUFF PASTRY

1 sheet frozen puff pastry 10-
  by 9-inches (thawed)
1 14-ounce wheel Brie cheese
2 4-ounce packages garlic and
  herb semi-soft cheese

1 egg, beaten
1 tablespoon water

Heat oven to 375°. Roll out pastry sheet on a lightly floured surface to remove fold line. Place brie in center of pastry. Spread one package semi-soft cheese on Brie. Turn Brie over and spread remaining semi-soft cheese on second side of Brie. Bring pastry up around side and over cheese, wrapping completely and trimming excess scraps. Re-roll scraps and cut out decorations to place on top of pastry if desired. Combine egg and water and brush over top. Bake pastry until golden brown, 30-35 minutes. Let stand 10 minutes. Serve warm.

Can be prepared one day ahead. Cover and refrigerate, bring to room temperature before baking.

Serves: 8 to 10.

$\mathscr{C}$HEESE DOLLARS

1/2 cup butter, softened
2 cups shredded sharp
  Cheddar cheese
1 1/2 cups flour

1/2 teaspoon salt
2 dashes of hot pepper
  sauce, or to taste
1/4 teaspoon paprika

Beat butter at medium speed of an electric mixer until creamy. Add cheese, , flour, paprika, hot pepper sauce and salt. Beat until mixture forms soft dough. Divide dough in half, shape into six-inch logs. Wrap in wax paper and chill. Cut logs into one-quarter inch slices and place on ungreased baking sheets. Bake at 350° for 10 to 12 minutes or until lightly brown. Cool one minute on sheets and transfer to cooling racks. Cool completely.

Yield: four dozen.

PARMESAN COOKIES

6 tablespoons flour
4 tablespoons butter, chilled
4 tablespoons freshly grated
Parmesan cheese

2 cloves chopped garlic
packed in oil (approximately 2 teaspoons or to taste)

Heat oven 350°. Process all ingredients in food processor until dough forms. Roll into a log about one and one-half inches in diameter. Chill until firm, about one hour. Slice dough one-quarter inch thick. Place two inches apart on cookie sheet. Bake for 10 minutes or until golden brown. Cool on wire rack.

Delicious alone, with wine or topped with pepper jelly.

Serves: eight.

SHRIMP LOUISIANA

1 pound medium or large
fresh shrimp
1/2 cup vinegar
20 bay leaves
2 medium size onions, sliced
2 cups corn oil

1/4 cup Worcestershire
sauce
1 teaspoon paprika
1/2 teaspoon cayenne
pepper
1/2 teaspoon salt

Clean and devein shrimp. Rinse in cold water and drain. Cook shrimp in boiling water three to four minutes. Drain and set aside. Heat the vinegar in a sauce pan with 10 bay leaves. Do not allow mixture to come to a boil. Remove bay leaves and set vinegar aside to cool. Layer shrimp, onion and bay leaves in a large jar or covered dish. Repeat until all has been used. Set aside. Mix vinegar, corn oil, Worcestershire sauce, paprika and cayenne. Pour over shrimp and set in refrigerator for at least eight hours. Serve with crackers.

Serves: eight.

$\mathscr{B}$LACK BEAN TORTE

1 2/3 cups dried black beans
6 cups vegetable or chicken
  broth
1 1/2 teaspoons ground
  cumin
3 cups slightly packed
  cilantro leaves
4 teaspoons olive oil
2 cloves garlic, minced or
  pressed

1/3 cup pine nuts
1 12-ounce jar roasted red
  peppers, rinsed and
  patted dry, then minced
  (put two tablespoons
  aside)
4 ounces crumbled feta
  cheese
1/2 cup plain yogurt or
  sour cream

Cook beans with cumin in the stock until they are tender. (If
you soak the beans overnight it reduces the cooking time.)
Drain thoroughly. Mash about one cup of the beans and mix
with remaining whole beans. Set aside and let cool. Line a 4-
by 8-inch loaf pan with plastic wrap, allowing the edges to
overlap the pan. Put half of the bean mixture into the pan,
gently pressing to make a smooth layer. Make cilantro pesto
by placing cilantro leaves, olive oil, garlic and pine nuts in a
food processor or blender and making puree. Carefully
spread the cilantro pesto over the beans. Make an even layer
of the peppers on top of the pesto. Sprinkle with the feta
cheese. Top cheese with the rest of the bean mixture, pressing
gently to make compact loaf. Cover tightly with plastic wrap
and chill at least four hours or up to three days, with something perched on top to add weight. Uncover pan, invert a
plate into it, and holding plate and pan together, invert again.
Lift pan off and remove plastic wrap. Spoon yogurt or sour
cream in a band down the middle of the loaf, and sprinkle
this with the reserved minced peppers. Present with several
knives or spatulas for serving with bread or crackers.

Yield: one loaf

SUN-DRIED TOMATO BITES

1/4 cup olive oil
2 cloves garlic, mashed
1 French bread baguette or
smaller twin loaves
12 ounces goat cheese (such as
Montrachet or Chévre)

1/4 cup sour cream
1/2 teaspoon of thyme
1/2 teaspoon rosemary
12 sun-dried tomatoes that
have been packed in oil
and drained

Heat oven to 425°. Crush garlic in oil. Thinly slice baguette. Lay bread on cookie sheet and brush with garlic oil, one side only. Bake until toasted. While they are baking, mix goat cheese with sour cream so that it is spreadable. Add rosemary and thyme. Finely chop the tomatoes. Take the bread out of the oven. Turn them over and place a layer of the cheese mixture on each slice and sprinkle with sun-dried tomatoes. Bake for three to five minutes and serve.

Yield: two dozen.

FRESH CORN SALSA

vegetable cooking spray
1 1/2 cup teaspoons
vegetable oil
10 sliced and divided green
onions
1 cup chopped unpeeled
tomato divided
1 cup corn cut from cob
(3 ears)

2 tablespoons chopped sweet
red pepper
2 tablespoons chopped green
pepper
1 minced clove garlic
2 teaspoons lime juice
1/4 teaspoons red pepper
1/4 teaspoon salt
1/4 teaspoon black pepper
garnish: green onion

Coat a large skillet with cooking spray; add oil and place over medium heat until hot. Add half of green onions, 3/4 cup tomato, corn, peppers and garlic. Cover and cook over low heat 15 minutes, stirring frequently. Remove from heat; stir in remaining green onions, remaining 1/4 cup tomato, lime juice and next three ingredients. Spoon into bowl. Garnish if desired. *Great as a side dish to grilled fish.*
Yield: 1 1/2 cups.

*M*ARINATED SHRIMP

2 pounds shrimp, boiled
  and peeled
1 8-ounce bottle seafood
  cocktail (or one cup
  ketchup mixed with two
  teaspoons horseradish)
1 1/2 cups mayonnaise

1 tablespoon Worcestershire
  sauce
2 onions, thinly sliced
1 teaspoon celery seed
1/4 teaspoon garlic salt
1 teaspoon hot pepper sauce
salt and pepper to taste

Mix all ingredients except shrimp. Stir well and add shrimp. Marinate six hours or longer. Serve with crackers.

Serves: six.

*M*USHROOM PÂTÉ

1 tablespoon butter or
  margarine
1/2 pound fresh mush-
  rooms, chopped
3 ounces cream cheese,
  softened

1/4 teaspoon garlic salt
1/4 teaspoon seasoned
  pepper
garnishes: fresh rosemary,
  sliced fresh mushrooms

Melt butter in a large skillet over medium heat. Add mushrooms. Cook, stirring often until all liquid is absorbed (about five minutes). Cool. Position knife blade in food processor bowl. Add mushrooms, cream cheese, garlic salt and pepper. Process until smooth, stopping occasionally to scrape down sides. Line a one-cup souffle dish with heavy-duty plastic wrap. Fill with mushroom mixture. Cover and chill. Unmold on a bed of greens and garnish with sliced mushrooms pressed around the bottom. Serve with toasted French baguette slices, melba rounds or water crackers.

Yield: one cup.

CRAB CAKES WITH LEMON DILL SAUCE

Crab Cakes
3 tablespoons butter
1 green onion, finely chopped
1 clove garlic, pressed
2 tablespoons finely chopped
  red bell pepper
cayenne pepper to taste
3 tablespoons heavy cream
1 tablespoon Dijon mustard
1 egg, beaten

1 teaspoon minced fresh
  basil
1 teaspoon minced fresh
  parsley
1 cup bread crumbs
1 pound fresh lump
  crabmeat, picked and
  cleaned
2 tablespoons oil
Lemon Dill Sauce (recipe
  follows)

Melt one tablespoon butter in large skillet and sauté onion, garlic and red pepper until wilted, about two minutes. Add cayenne, cream and Dijon mustard. Cool slightly. Add beaten egg, basil, parsley, half cup bread crumbs and crabmeat. Mix lightly. Mold into 16 two-inch wide patties. Put one-half cup remaining bread crumbs in shallow dish. Roll patties in crumbs. Chill at least one hour. Combine oil and remaining two tablespoons butter over moderate heat in large skillet. Sauté crab cakes three minutes on each side. Serve with Lemon Dill Sauce.

Lemon Dill Sauce
3/4 cup mayonnaise
1/2 cup buttermilk
2 tablespoons chopped fresh
  dill
1 tablespoon minced parsley

2 teaspoons fresh lemon
  juice
1 tablespoon grated lemon
  peel
1 clove garlic, pressed

Combine all ingredients in medium bowl. Chill until mixture thickens.

Cakes can be made early in day and refrigerated before cooking.

Yield: 16 cakes.

ASSAIL

6 sticks cinnamon	1 teaspoon bitters
16 whole cloves	1/4 cup rum (or one teaspoon
1 teaspoon ground allspice	rum flavoring)
1/4 cup sugar	
2 cups cranberry juice	
1 12 ounce can frozen apple	
juice, diluted with six	
cups water	

Tie spices together in cloth bag. Combine sugar, juices and bitters. Simmer 10 minutes and remove bag. Add rum or flavoring last.

Can be prepared stove top or in drip or percolator coffee maker. Wonderful holiday beverage. Easily doubled for crowd.

Serves: eight.

$\mathcal{E}$GGNOG ELAINE

2 pints coffee ice cream	1 cup bourbon
2 quarts eggnog, chilled	2 cups whipping cream
3 cups coffee, cold	nutmeg

Scoop ice cream into 10 large balls, place on non-stick pan and freeze 24 hours. Stir eggnog, coffee and bourbon into large chilled punch bowl. Whip cream in medium bowl to soft peaks. Fold into eggnog mixture. Place ice cream balls on top and sprinkle lightly with nutmeg. Serve at once.

Yield: 15 cups.

ALMOND TEA

2 tablespoons lemon-
flavored instant ice-tea
mix
2 cups hot water
1 1/2 cups sugar
10 cups water, divided

1 12-ounce can frozen pine-
apple-orange-banana drink
concentrate, thawed and
undiluted
1 1/2 teaspoons almond
extract

Combine tea mix and hot water, stirring until tea mix dissolves; set aside. Combine sugar and two cups water in a Dutch oven. Bring to a boil. Boil five minutes. Stir in tea mixture, remaining eight cups water, frozen drink concentrate, and almond extract. Chill. Serve over ice and garnish with sliced oranges or lemons and mint.

Yield: three quarts.

FLORIDA SUNRISE

1 12-ounce can frozen
orange juice concentrate,
thawed and undiluted
1 12-ounce can apricot
nectar, chilled
1 1/2 pints commercial
strawberry sorbet,
softened

3 cups water
1 (750 milliliter) bottle
alcoholic or non-alcoholic
variety champagne, chilled
3 cups crushed ice
Garnish: whole fresh
strawberries

Combine orange juice, apricot nectar, sorbet and water in a large container. Stir until blended. Chill. To serve, pour mixture into a punch bowl. Stir in champagne and ice. Serve in stemmed glasses, and garnish, if desired.

To make ahead: combine first four ingredients a day ahead of time; chill. Add champagne and ice just before serving.

Yield: one gallon.

COFFEE VELVET

10 whole cloves
2 cinnamon sticks, broken in
  half
3/4 cup ground coffee
1/4 cup sugar

10 cups cold water
1/2 cup whipped heavy
  cream
ground cinnamon for
  garnish

Place cloves, cinnamon sticks and coffee in brew basket of automatic drip coffeemaker. Place sugar in carafe of coffee maker. Brew coffee. Serve hot or cold over ice in mugs or cups. Top with whipped cream and dust with cinnamon.

Wonderful after dinner treat!

Yields: 10 cups.

CAFÉ CON LECHE

1 quart milk
4 cups water
1/3 - 1/2 cup instant coffee
powder or granules

1/3 cup sugar
ground cinnamon (optional)

Just before serving in 3-quart saucepan over medium-high heat, heat milk and water until hot (do not boil). Stir in instant coffee and sugar until dissolved. Pour in cups. Sprinkle each serving with cinnamon if desired.

Serves: 8 to10.

BOUGAINVILLEA

1/3 cup champagne
1/3 cup orange juice

1/3 cup cranberry juice

Mix champagne, orange juice and cranberry juice. Pour over ice and serve. Delicious for brunch.

Serves: two.

CIDER GROG

1/2 gallon cider
3/4 cup brown sugar
1/2 teaspoon ground all-
spice
1/2 teaspoon cloves, ground
1/2 teaspoon cinnamon

1/2 teaspoon nutmeg
2 cups golden or dark rum
(optional)
2 oranges, thinly sliced
2 lemons, thinly sliced
cinnamon sticks

Blend the cider, brown sugar and spices in a large pan and simmer 15 minutes or until sugar is dissolved. Add rum, if desired, and oranges and lemons. Stir and simmer two minutes more. Serve in cups garnished with cinnamon sticks.

Yield: 8 to 12 cups.

CAPPUCCINO

3/4 cup instant Espresso
coffee powder
1 ounce unsweetened
chocolate, chopped
4 cups water
4 tablespoons sugar

4 cups milk
1 cup heavy or whipping
cream
1/2 teaspoon vanilla
ground cinnamon

About 30 minutes before serving in a four quart sauce pan over high heat, heat instant Espresso, chocolate, water and three tablespoons of sugar until chocolate melts, sugar dissolves and mixture boils. Stir occasionally. Add milk and cook over medium heat until tiny bubbles form around edge and mixture is hot. Stir occasionally. (Beat heavy or whipping cream, vanilla extract and one tablespoon sugar in a small bowl with mixer at medium speed until soft peaks form.) To serve, with wire whisk, beat hot Espresso mixture until foamy; pour into cups. Top each serving with cinnamon.

Unsweetened chocolate is the secret ingredient in this easy cappuccino recipe, made without a fancy, expensive machine.

Serves: four.

Preceding Page: Brunch With the Old City House Inn and Restaurant. Menu: See Page 241

Beach sunrises are among the most beautiful sights in the Jacksonville area. Amelia Island, with its many resorts and sandy beaches, offers natural delights to natives and tourists alike.

After Henry Flagler popularized Jacksonville in the late 1800's, winter visitors flocked to enjoy her balmy and sandy beaches. The old boardwalk at Jacksonville Beach offered hours of entertainment whether socializing or strolling along watching the ocean panorama.

Photograph is from collections at The Beaches Area Historical Society.

§

Gator Burgers

Cracker Veggies on a Stick With a Kick *

Boiled Green Peanuts

San Jose Pasta Salad *

Root Beer

Fat Man Cakes *

§

Round up a posse of fellers for a cowpoke birthday party Jacksonville style. (Jacksonville was originally named Cowford, because it was located where cattle drives crossed the St. Johns.) Handmade invitations are rolled up and tied with jute or rope suggesting that the boys arrive in cowboy duds. Straw hats and bandannas are provided as favors! A neighborhood park or riding stable is the perfect place for such an event. Bales of hay, old quilts and rusty buckets add to the experience of an encounter with ole time "Florida crackers." A trick-roper or whip-cracker is secured for entertainment. Seed spitting and horseshoe tossing are a must! Everyone circles up for cake and there is an ole fashioned story-tellin' before the gifts are unwrapped.

§

"Croc Tails" — Grilled Hotdogs on a Stick

Assorted Chips

Skewered Fresh Fruit

Swamp-colored Punch Served From a Large Metal Pot

Sour Cream Chocolate Cake and Frosting *

§

" **G** 'Day Mate!" Join us on a "walkabout" with crocs and snakes. No youngster can refuse this invitation! The guests congregate "outback" behind the host's home and find an array of rustic decor; burlap sacks, wooden crates, yellow and green balloons, boomerangs and life size kangaroos made of cardboard. A professional reptile handler from St. Augustine captivates the audience with a very educational show displaying various reptiles, including an alligator that everyone has an opportunity to pet. Sack races and three-legged relays are enjoyed as well as a "joey-toss." A lightweight basketball hoop is mounted on the pouch of a cardboard kangaroo cutout, and by tossing the foam ball, or Joey, the children win sacks of trail mix. Each child leaves with a picture of himself with the alligator and a camouflage bag filled with gummy worms, candy bugs and creepy crawlers.

§

Creamy Tomato Spread With Crackers *

Popcorn

Hot Ham Sandwiches *

Sheet Cake With a Poodle Design

Ice Cream Sodas

§

The young party goers are requested to arrive at the skating rink dressed in Fifties style. The poodle skirts, ponytails and bobby socks add to the decorations of pastel colored balloons, crepe paper streamers, jukebox cut-outs, and 45s (records). As the girls are putting on their skates, they apply bright red lipstick and chiffon scarves for added emphasis. The music, of course, includes songs from the 50s as well as some of the favorite current tunes. A designated photographer takes an instant picture of each child. Guests are sent home with their picture and a goodie bag decorated with pink poodles, filled with jacks, bubble gum, plastic bangle bracelets and assorted candy.

§

Wedding Cake

Lemon Velvet Ice Cream *

Sparkling Apple Juice

§

What six or seven year old girl doesn't like to dress up in her mother's frilly prom dress? Each guest arrives at "the ball" and finds gold and silver balloons, stars that sparkle and metallic confetti everywhere. The birthday girl is dressed as Cinderella complete with crown and two wicked step-sisters. The mother is the fairy godmother with a wand and robe. Dad charms the guest as the handsome prince or a pumpkin (depending on his mood)! A coach, drawn by a beautiful horse and coachman is secured from someone who handles wedding arrangements. Four or five girls at a time tour the neighborhood. Those waiting play musical chairs around a pumpkin or "pin the slipper on the foot." Party favors are wrapped in metallic netting. Each guest leaves with a helium filled gold or silver balloon.

§

Braised Atlantic Grouper Over Warm White Asparagus

Tat-soi Salad With Truffle Oil Vinaigrette

Ferrari Carano Chardonnay 1992

Fresh Melon Parisian With Campari

Seared Herb Crust Veal Loin With Hazelnut Menuiere

Roast Shallot Potato Gateau

Robert Mondavi Cabernet Reserve 1987

Créme Brûleé Miramar With Fresh Berries *

Moet et Chandon Demi Sec

§

24 Miramar is just the place to celebrate that special occasion be it New Year's Eve, a birthday or simply a romantic evening. The tables are set with crisp white linens. Soft candlelight and flowers set the mood. The service is impeccable. It has achieved that impossible balance of being attentive without being intrusive. As each course arrives, you regret that you don't have a camera to record it. An artist has balanced the colors and textures, as well as the positioning of the food. You savor each bite knowing that this experience is as close to divine as you can get.

Holiday Brunch

§

Creamed Shrimp With Chipotle Sauce Over English Muffins *

Pear Halves Baked With Orange Marmalade and Toasted Almonds

Honey-baked Ham

Chunky Chocolate Cherry Bread *

Cinnamon Popovers *

Lemon, Chocolate, Cranberry Cheesecake *

Gingerbread Roll With Lemon Filling *

Mamie's Chocolate Cherries *

Wassail *

Eggnog Elaine *

§

Whether at home or in such a lovely place as the Cummer Art Museum, the fragrance of fresh evergreens and the lush beauty of poinsettias greet visitors with the warmth of the season. Gilded angels and pine cones or fruit are accented by deep red roses and velvet ribbons that reflect in the silver, giving off a warm glow to the lavishly laden table. A harpist plays carols or the hostess may choose to softly fill the room with the music of *Handel's Messiah*. As the guests leave, they are sent home with a memorable ornament wrapped in gold paper.

Candlelight Dinner

§

Marinated Shrimp *

Ortega Company Salad With Raspberry Vinaigrette *

Sirloin With Green Peppercorn Sauce *

Asparagus in Squash Rings *

River City Rolls *

Amy's Frozen Raspberry Souffle *

§

*Q*uiet, intimate dinners don't have to be elaborate to be exquisite. The simplicity of silver and linen adorned by candlesticks of various heights and sizes is breathtaking. A spouse or boyfriend surprised with this special meal is sure to be forever impressed. A mysterious invitation delivered to the office is just the thing. Of course, children are "farmed out," the dog fed, lights dimmed and champagne chilled.

§

Spiced Nuts *

Sliced Tequila Tenderloin *

New Wave Salad *

Nancy's Veggie Relish Served in a Purple Cabbage *

Dried Cherry Muffins *

Layered Shortbread *

§

As the Jacksonville Zoo grows to become the pride of this region, why not experience the wild with a group of friends. Whatever the setting, decorations reminiscent of Africa provide the unexpected. The exquisite simplicity of Herend figurines combined with other wildlife candlesticks, napkin rings and tablecloths enhance the setting. A collection of children's toys, i.e. zebras, elephants and giraffes, work well with a loose arrangement of dried flowers and raffia. Each guest receives a bit of trivia about a different designated animal and all are encouraged to find the exhibit with their animal. Don't forget the camera!

Tailgate at the TPC

§

Chilled Raspberry Soup *

Salmon Loaf With Dill Sauce *

English Cucumber & Potato Salad *

Carribean Carrots *

Almond Tea *

Blackbottom Cupcakes *

Nutmeg Ice Box Cookies *

Mother Magee's Mandarin Orange Cookies *

§

Tailgate parties are not just for football anymore. Certainly, the Jacksonville Jaguars may draw their share of hungry fans, but spring at the Tournament Players Championship is hard to beat. Surprise your guests with this beautiful menu. The picnic is transported in sealed plastic containers but served from lucite bowls, enamelware and pewter. Fresh fruit and parsley are tasteful garnishes. The raspberry soup is served from a halved melon. Clay pots are stacked with sheet moss making a wonderful candelabrum and small pots are used as votive candles. Potted flowers also wrapped with sheet moss add warmth to the festivities. Save the dishes for later, just wrap in plastic bags for the ride home. Enjoy!

A Southern Game Supper

§

Warm Blue Cheese and Bacon Dip *

Lemon Pheasant *

Wild Rice

Cranberry Sausage Tartlets *

Julie's One Hour Baguette *

Heart of Palm Salad *

Rhubarb, Apple and Pineapple Pie *

Coffee Velvet *

§

The strong Southern heritage of Jacksonville is still very much evident in the architecture, dialect and cuisine of many of her citizens. Hunting is still enjoyed, but whether your family brings home the game for supper or not, the experience of eating venison, game birds, or pheasant is both delicious and memorable. Magnolia blossoms and leaves are readily available and are lovely centerpieces combined with huge brass candelabrum and red berries. Framed photographs of ancestors generate wonderful conversation and humor as your guests discuss family traditions and memories.

§

Stuffed Tomatillos

Cheese Chilies

Peach Margaritas

Spinach Salad With Rosewood Strawberry Dressing *

Chili Blanco *

Bunny's Carrot Cake *

Café Con Leche *

§

*M*ost newcomers to Jacksonville agree that Southern hospitality makes this an inviting place to call home. This luncheon menu for new neighbors is sure to generate conversation and develop friendships. Invitations are handwritten on brown paper and tied with raffia to a bottle of hot pepper sauce. The front door is decorated with a wreath of dried chilies or fresh chili peppers. Guests are greeted with a wooden platter of chili-spiked cheese tidbits molded in the shape of chilies and stuffed tomatillos. Margaritas for midday are created by omitting the alcohol and adding peaches. Beverages are served in salt-rimmed glasses with a sliced lime for garnish. The guests are seated by place cards which are brown-paper wrapped boxes of dried bean soup mix or chili seasoning packets-tied with raffia. As the meal progresses everyone shares something "spicy" from their past. If things haven't already heated up enough, serve coffee and cake that has been garnished with almond paste formed into the shape of nothing less than chili peppers!

§

Voodoo Shrimp and Crawfish *

Red Beans and Rice *

Gumbo *

Crawfish Etouffee *

Beignets

§

In keeping with its Cajun theme, Ragtime celebrates the Mardi Gras in a grand manner. This Atlantic Beach restaurant is always bustling, so it is not hard to imagine those crazy days in New Orleans. Decorations produce a carnival-type atmosphere. Balloons, jewelry, trinkets and coins spill over the tables. Guests are invited to come in costume complete with masks.

§

Orange Spritzer

Tomato Juice Cocktail

Mixed Greens With Citrus and Honey Dressing *

Spinach Salad With Roasted Garlic Vinaigrette *

Baked Garlic and Cheese Grits *

Seven Herb Fried Eggs *

Asparagus With Cashew Butter *

Fillet Medallions With Poached Eggs and Asparagus Tips
and Cream Cheese Hollandaise *

Assorted Bread Sticks

Glazed Peaches and Cream

Hazelnut Cookies

§

Celebrate a special occasion with brunch at Old City House Inn and Restaurant. Located in downtown St. Augustine, in the heart of the Historic District, the restaurant reminds visitors of the comfortable elegance of the seventeenth century. Built in 1873, the Inn once served as a stable for the Ammidown Mansion which was located on St. George Street. In 1896, the buildings were renovated and became one of the winter cottages rented to wealthy Northerners. This five room Bed and Breakfast Inn is one of St. Augustine's finest examples of Colonial Revival style architecture.

Poolside Party

§

Florida Sunrise *

Crab Cakes with Lemon Dill Sauce *

Black Bean Torte *

Tangy Shrimp Kabobs *

Fresh Corn Salsa *

White Rice

Crusty French Bread

Frozen Orange Custards *

Light French White Bordeaux

§

As the lazy, hazy days of summer linger on, it's nice to treat yourself and friends to a special evening outside . Entertaining outdoors means a casual atmosphere. Hand written invitations with a beach or pool theme are sent to the guests. Food is prepared ahead of time, so the hostess can relax and enjoy the party. As guests arrive they are greeted at the door with cool Florida Sunrises. Each guest is handed a pair of crazy "cool shades" to wear until the sun goes down. The buffet and dining tables are draped in brightly colored table skirts. Centerpieces consist of three six to eight inch terra cotta pots planted with bright tropical flowers. Pots are wrapped in sheet moss and the top band is decorated with small shells. Votive candles are randomly placed around the flower pots. Place cards are made of three inch terra cotta pots filled with sand. A paper umbrella bearing a flag with the guest's name is stuck in the sand and shells are scattered on top. Beverages are chilled and placed in large terra cotta pots lined with plastic bags and filled with ice. Coordinating bright color table and dinnerware are used. And of course, what pool party would be complete without the citronella tiki torches?

The Age of Elegance: A Tribute to the Cummers

§

Artichoke Stuffed With Marinated Prawns

Champagne Vinaigrette With Aioli Mayonnaise

Mixed Baby Greens With Sliced Grilled Duck Breast and Raspberry Vinaigrette

Fillet of Beef with Madeira Wine Mushroom Sauce

Burgundy Truffle and Bernaise Sauces

Fresh Green Asparagus

Scalloped Potatoes

Variety of Fresh Baked Breads

Raspberry English Trifle and Petit Chocolate Gateau With Almond Creme

§

The shimmer and sparkle of crystal chandeliers ... the crisp charm and formality of black and white ... exquisite lace and wide sashes ... full-length gloves and ostrich feather fans ... discreet assignations in the orangery.

The Age of Elegance reflects the life and times of Arthur and Ninah Cummer. The Cummers came to Jacksonville in 1897. In the early 1900s, they built a Tudor Revival Mansion on Riverside. Later, the riverfront property was transformed into a formal English garden. This garden was later expanded in the Italian style with terraces, nooks, sculptures and reflecting pools. Family tragedy led the Cummers to pursue the collection of art. These paintings and the gardens were the gift of a generous family to the people of Jacksonville.

The Augustine Room / Marriott at Sawgrass

The Augustine Room is an elegant, intimate restaurant tucked into the Marriott at Sawgrass Resort. It is a five-star restaurant that is very European in ambience. With candle-light and fresh flowers, the Augustine Room is romance inspiring. To dine in the Augustine Room is to be pampered. The Executive Chef, Chet Surmaczewicz was chosen by his peers as 1994 Southeast Regional Chef of the Year. He also has served as the president of the American Culinary Federation, St. Augustine Chapter.

CHICKEN WRAPPED LOBSTER

Served With a Yellow and Purple Pepper Relish

4 6-ounce chicken breasts	1 quart chicken stock
4 3-ounce lobster tails	1 cup sherry
4 ounces sweet corn	yellow & purple pepper
1/2 red pepper, julienne	relish (recipe follows)
salt and pepper, to taste	

Take the chicken breast, pound lightly to create even thickness. Place the lobster down the center of the chicken breast. Top with sweet corn and julienne red pepper. Salt and pepper. Wrap the chicken breast around the lobster tail tightly. Wrap in plastic wrap and aluminum foil. Poke six to seven holes with fork. Place in room temperature chicken stock and sherry. Bring to a simmer (approximately 170°-180°) for approximately 25-30 minutes. Check temperature (internal), it should be 150°-160°. Slice and serve over relish.

Yellow & Purple Pepper
 Relish
1/2 yellow pepper

1/2 purple pepper
1/2 cup corn
4 ounces Vinaigrette dressing

Dice peppers and mix ingredients. Season with salt and pepper.

$\mathcal{H}$ONEY GLAZED BATTEN ISLAND PORK CHOPS

4 8-ounce center cut pork
 chops
6 ounces honey
1/4 cup Batten Island mild
1 fresh peach, sliced 1/4
 inch thick
1/8 cup malt vinegar

1/8 cup Worcestershire
 sauce
1/4 cup diced onions
4 ounces salad oil
peach and onion marma-
 lade (recipe follows)

Combine the honey, Batten Island mild, peach, malt vinegar, worcestershire sauce, onions and salad oil. Use this mixture to marinade the pork chops overnight. Grill over low flame to internal temperature of 160°. Serve with the peach and onion marmalade.

Honey glazed center cut pork chops with peach and onion marmalade.

Peach and Onion Marmalade

1 onion, sliced thin
1/4 cup Batten Island mild
1 cup orange juice

2 peaches sliced, 1/4 inch
 thick

Saute all the ingredients in a nonstick pan until tender.

EAR CHUTNEY

8 ounces Mango chutney
1 pear, diced into medium-
 sized cubes

1 teaspoon Batten Island
 mild

Mix all the ingredients. Serve with steak.

$\mathscr{S}$TEAK MARINADE

2 tablespoons Batten Island
hot
1/4 teaspoon Chinese five
spice
4 cloves garlic, crushed

pinch lemon pepper
1/4 teaspoon Worcestershire
sauce
1/4 teaspoon basil

Combine the ingredients and use a marinade for steak.

$\mathscr{S}$AUTEED PORK LOIN
With Banana Chutney

8 4-ounce pork loin
medallions
1 banana, chopped
2 ounces banana liquor
4 ounces oil
salt and pepper

1 cup chopped banana
2 ounces mild chicken stock
1 teaspoon Batten Island
sauce
banana chutney (recipe
follows)

Combine the banana, banana liquor, oil and seasoning. Marinade the medallions overnight with this mixture. Sear the medallions for one minute on each side in a nonstick pan.

Place in a roasting pan. Place one cup of chopped bananas over the top of the medallions. Add the chicken stock to bottom of pan with one teaspoon Batten Island sauce. Place in oven at 325° until internal temperature reaches 160°. Serve with banana chutney.

Banana Chutney
8 ounces plain chutney
1 banana sliced

Combine the ingredients.

The Beech Street Grill is located near the heart of historical Fernandina Beach on Amelia Island. The restaurant, known for its somewhat eclectic New American cuisine, is in a quaint turn-of-the century home. A fusion menu revolves around fresh seafood and the finest available regional ingredients. An impressive wine cellar of over four thousand bottles compliments the cuisine. The Beech Street Grill is committed to quality, consistency and creativity.

SAUTEED SOFTSHELL CRAB
With Red Pepper Butter Sauce and Andouille Provencale

1 cup milk
1/2 cup flour
1/2 cup white cornmeal
1 teaspoon salt
1/2 teaspoon pepper
softshell crabs
red pepper butter sauce
    (recipe follows)

3 ounces Andouille sausage, chopped
4 ounces tomato concasse
2 ounces sliced mushrooms
2 scallions, chopped
1/2 teaspoon garlic, chopped
1 ounce white wine

Prepare red pepper butter sauce. Rinse crab, remove gills. Soak crab in milk. Stir the dry mix together. Lightly dust crab on both sides. Saute the crab in hot oil. Cook both sides, one to two minutes per side. Remove the crab and drain on paper towels. Use pan to make Andouille provencale. Deglaze pan with white wine. Add remaining ingredients. Cook down until wine is gone. Transfer crab to plate. Sauce with red pepper butter sauce, top with Andouille provencale. Garnish with fresh chopped scallions.

Red Pepper Butter Sauce

1 medium onion
2 ears corn, cooked
2-4 ounces butter
12 ounces red bell pepper,
  roasted

1 pint heavy cream
salt and white pepper, to taste
cumin to taste
cayenne pepper, to taste

Saute onions in two ounces butter. Add cooked corn, cut off the cob. Add salt, pepper, cumin and cayenne. Stir in the roasted red peppers. Cook briefly. Stir in four ounces heavy cream. Bring to a boil. Remove from fire. Puree in blender or food processor, return to fire. Add more heavy cream to desired thickness. Bring to boil and remove from heat. Stir in remaining whole butter.

$\mathcal{G}$RILLED YELLOWFIN TUNA
With Kalamata Tapenade and Dilled Cream Sauce

yellowfin tuna
kalamata tapenade (recipe
  follows)

dilled cream (recipe
  follows)

Prepare the tapenade and dill cream. Grill tuna to desired doneness. Pipe alternating sauces onto fish, cornrow pattern. Garnish with a sprig of fresh dill.

Kalamata Tapenade

4 ounces kalamata (Greek)
  olives, rinsed and pitted
2 cloves garlic, roasted
3 anchovies, rinsed

2 tablespoons capers, rinsed
1 ounce rum
olive oil

Soak olives, capers and anchovies in rum after rinsing. Puree all in food processor. Drizzle in olive oil to desired consistency. (Keep thick in order to pipe onto fish.)

Dilled Cream

2 tablespoons shallots
3 tablespoons chopped dill
1 ounce white vinegar

3 ounces white wine
1/2 teaspoon white pepper
4 ounces creme fraiche (sour cream)

In a saucepan, reduce white wine and vinegar with shallots, dill and pepper. Cook down until almost dry. Remove from heat. Let cool. Fold in creme fraiche. Chill.

HERB-CRUSTED GROUPER
With Wild Mushroom Crabmeat Ragout

8 ounce grouper fillet
1 bunch tarragon
1 bunch basil
1 bunch chives
1/2 bunch parsley
1/2 bunch dill
2 cups fresh ground bread crumbs

1/2 red onion, chopped very fine
4 ounces butter, melted
mushroom crabmeat ragout (recipe follows)

Chop all herbs. Mix in finely chopped bread crumbs and onion. Drizzle with melted butter. Reserve. Prepare the ragout. Bake the fillet on sizzler platter with wine and lemon juice until nearly done. Remove from oven and pack on herb-bread crumb mixture. Return to oven until crust is golden brown and fish is cooked. Top with mushroom ragout.

Mushroom Crabmeat Ragout

4 ounces chanterelles, oyster, shiitake and/or wood ear mushrooms
3 ounces lump crabmeat
1 tablespoon butter
2 ounces white wine
3 ounces demi-glace
2 ounces heavy cream
1/2 bunch chives
salt and pepper, to taste
2 tablespoons chopped shallots

Quarter mushrooms. Saute´ lightly in butter. Add the shallots and season with salt and pepper. Moisten with wine. Add the heavy cream. Bring to a boil and simmer one to two minutes. Add demi-glace, bring to a quick boil, remove from fire. Fold in crabmeat, chopped chives. Keep warm.

*B*ROILED SNAPPER

With Mango-Melon and Sour Cherry Sauce and Grilled Pineapple Salsa

8 ounce snapper filet
Grilled Pineapple Salsa
(recipe follows)
Mango Melon Sauce
(recipe follows)
Sour Cherry Sauce
(recipe follows)

Prepare the grilled pineapple salsa and chill. Prepare the mango melon and sour cherry sauces. Broil the fillet on sizzler platter in white wine and lemon juice. Place the cooked filet on plate. Ladle mango sauce over fish. Carefully pipe lines of sour cherry sauce over mango sauce. Spoon small amount of grilled pineapple salsa and serve.

Grilled Pineapple Salsa

1 tablespoon oil
1 pineapple, sliced lengthwise into 1/4 inch slices
1/2 red onion, chopped
2 tablespoons brown sugar
1 red bell pepper, chopped

2 tablespoons cilantro,
  chopped
juice of 1 lime
2 tablespoons red wine
  vinegar
1/2 bunch scallions, chopped

Grill pineapple and dice. Sauté onion in oil. Add brown sugar, cook briefly with red bell pepper. Fold in remaining ingredients. Refrigerate until one hour before serving.

Mango Melon Sauce

1 ripe cantaloupe
2 ripe mangos
1 ancho chili
1/2 red onion
2 tablespoons brown sugar

2 tablespoons butter
2 tablespoons orange juice
  concentrate
  (or zest of 1 orange)
4 ounces heavy cream

Sauté onion in butter. Add chopped chilies, mangos and cantaloupe. Cook briefly. Add brown sugar, orange juice and cook for three to five minutes. Remove from fire and puree in blender or food processor.

Sour Cherry Sauce

2 teaspoons oil
1/2 red onion
2 tablespoons brown sugar
1 cup sour cherries, pureed

2 tablespoons apple blossom
  honey
2 tablespoons plum wine

Sauté onion in oil. Add brown sugar, sour cherries and plum wine. Cook until thick. Remove from fire and puree. Stir in honey. Strain through fine sieve into ketchup squirt bottle. Hold in hot water bath until ready to serve.

Cafe on the Square is located in the heart of historic San Marco. It is housed in the first commercially built structure in San Marco. Needless to say, this 1926 building is a registered landmark. The restaurant's interior is dark and rustic with wooden beams and visible brickwork. Cafe on the Square was established in 1984 and continues to be quite the evening gathering spot. The food is upbeat and freshly prepared. Some of the specialties include chicken Captiva, coconut shrimp, fresh seafood, salads and gourmet pita pizza.

RASPBERRY SHIITAKE FILET

A fillet stuffed with sauteed shitake mushrooms and served with a raspberry-Pinot Noir-Shiraz sauce.

4 8-ounce filets
(cut almost in half)
1/4 cup cold water
1 3/4 cups Shiraz wine
1 1/2 cups Pinot Noir
(Cabernet does nicely)
1 pint fresh raspberries
1 pound fresh shiitake
mushrooms (black
Japanese mushrooms)

2 tablespoons sugar (or
to taste)
3/4 cup finely diced shallots
(small sweet onions)
4 cloves garlic, minced
(fresh is better)
2 tablespoons olive oil
(extra virgin or virgin)
salt and pepper, to taste

Over low heat, cook the raspberries, water and sugar for eight to 10 minutes then add the Shiraz and Pinot Noir and reduce by half. Stir frequently. Maintain low heat throughout reduction process to avoid scorching. When mixture is reduced by half the amount started with and it coats the back of spoon, remove from heat and strain through cheesecloth or a very fine mesh strainer, to capture all the seeds. Set aside for future use. In a medium-sized sauce pan, heat olive oil over medium to high heat until it begins to smoke slightly. Then, add shiitake mushrooms. Sauté until limp over medium heat. Add garlic, salt and pepper. Sauté until shallots are translucent. Set aside for future use. Prepare grill on medium to high setting and place the filets on the grill (make sure the proportional cut is made before grilling) to desired temperatures stuff each filet with one-quarter of the mushroom mixture (heated), pour one-quarter of the raspberry sauce (heated) over each filet and garnish with fresh raspberries and parsley sprigs.

Mushroom mixture and raspberry sauce can be prepared ahead of time and refrigerated. Remember that the mixture and sauce must be reheated slowly over low-medium heat.

Serves: four

Cafe Carmon

Cafe Carmon is a trendy cafe that started off specializing in soup, salads, sandwiches, pastas and desserts. It developed quite a following for its desserts. Several years ago, Cafe Carmon expanded its menu to include dinner items such as chicken San Marco, goat cheese salad, baked Brie, grilled salmon salad and Black Angus beef. The Executive Chef is Michael McBride and the Pastry Chef is Patty Hay. The cafe is located in an old building in San Marco. The cafe's design features two slightly different levels and an interesting room divider of glass panes. The walls are hung with Impressionist prints. Outside dining is available as well. Cafe Carmon is still a great place to go for late night dessert and coffee.

GRILLED SALMON
With Tomato Salsa and Tarragon-Honey Mustard

4 - 8 ounce salmon filets
4 ripe medium tomatoes, diced
1 bunch scallion, chopped
1 red onion, diced
1 jalapeno, diced

1 small bunch cilantro
juice of one lemon chopped
1 teaspoon garlic powder
salt, to taste
tarragon-honey mustard
(recipe follows)

Prepare the salsa by combining the tomatoes, scallions, red onions, jalapeno, lemon juice, cilantro and garlic powder. Season with salt and mix well. Set aside. Prepare the mustard. Grill the salmon until done. Place in the middle of each plate. Spoon some of the salsa on each side of the salmon and top with the tarragon-honey mustard.

Tarragon-Honey Mustard
1 cup Dijon mustard

1/2 cup honey
1 tablespoon tarragon

Add all the ingredients together and mix well.

Serves: four.

This Jacksonville Beach restaurant combines European ambience with a casual beach attitude. Hans' Bistro has been serving this area for 15 years and is a favorite of some of the Tournament Players Championship set. Featured dishes include Hungarian goulash, German sauerbraten, rack of lamb and wiener schnitzel. Hans Kaunath, who is the Chef and owner, is German trained. His work has taken him to Stockholm, London, on a cruise line traveling to South America, to Bermuda, to Nassau, Bahamas before he settled in the Ponte Vedra area.

GERMAN POTATO PANCAKES

4 large potatoes, peeled   1 teaspoon chopped parsley
1 medium onion, chopped   salt and pepper, to taste
1 egg

Grate the potatoes. Add the chopped onion, egg, parsley, salt and pepper. Mix well. Heat a large frying pan and add a small amount of oil. Spread potato mixture into pancake-sized shapes and brown on both sides.

Serves: four.

WIENER SCHNITZEL

6 ounces veal cutlet,   egg
  pounded thin   breading

Dredge in flour, egg and breading, in that order. Heat a frying pan with a mixture of oil and butter (about two tablespoons). Brown the cutlet on both sides and serve with lemon.

The Metro Diner is located on Hendricks Avenue just south of historic San Marco. It occupies the same site that a neighborhood "short order" diner once did. The diner's charmingly quaint atmosphere is enhanced by an herb and flower garden. Metro Diner is known for its delicious yet health-conscious fare. Jeff Stermer, a Culinary Institute of America Graduate, and Clint Ross, prepare dishes that range from vegetarian cuisine to crêpes de jour and omelettes. Amazingly, the Metro is open seven days a week from 7 a.m. to 10 p.m.

PAN FRIED SEA TROUT
With Caper Cream Sauce

8 ounces filet of sea trout
1 ounce finely diced onion
1 ounce capers in brine
4 ounces heavy cream

2 ounces white wine
pinch black pepper
pinch granulated garlic
flour to dredge

Dredge the fish in flour and place in the pan with a little oil over low heat. The fish should be skin side up. When the fish is golden in color, turn the fish and continue to cook. When the fish is nearly done (about 10 minutes), put onions and capers in the pan to sauté. When the onions are transparent, add wine to the pan to deglaze. Remove the fish and add cream to the wine, onions and capers. Add the pepper and garlic. When the cream is thickened, pour sauce over the fish and serve.

24 Miramar is uniquely different. Many consider it the best restaurant in Jacksonville. The ambience is chic, yet elegant and understated. On a typical night, the tables might be decorated with simple, sophisticated arrangements of orchids. 24 Miramar's cutting edge cuisine is visually appealing. Among featured dishes are Veal Miramar which is veal medallions with wild mushrooms in port, as well as an entree of Shrimp and Goat Cheese Capellini. Maybe it's Chef Brian Clayton's Disney Culinary training, but the team at 24 Miramar consider the desires of the guests to be more important than being true to the accepted standards of cuisine.

CREME BRULEE MIRAMAR

10 egg yolks
2 3/4 cups heavy cream
1 vanilla bean pod, split
3 ounces sugar

4 ounces light brown sugar
1 sheet puff pastry
fresh berries

Heat heavy cream and vanilla (in husk) in a sauce pan to not quite boiling. Remove from heat. In a double boiler, whisk together egg yolks and sugar constantly until it is a firm froth. Add the cream mixture to eggs and cook for approximately 25 minutes until thickened. Remove the vanilla bean husks and refrigerate. Cut the pastry sheet into six equal squares and place into very large muffin tins with a coffee filter on top of each. Gently push the pastry into the tins and fill with coffee beans to hold in place. Bake at 350° until light brown. Remove the beans and break off the edges to leave a cup shaped pastry dish. Cover the bottom of the pastry cup with fresh fruit slices and fill with the egg mixture to very top of the cup. Sprinkle completely with brown sugar and broil on the top rack for a few seconds to caramelize. (A butane torch will produce a better result.) Garnish with fresh berries and serve proudly.

This rich dessert has turned many a chocoholic's head with it's ability to provide all the richness and depth of flavor using only vanilla.

The Old City House is a popular destination in St. Augustine. The restaurant is a charmingly restored 19th-century home. It can best be described as cozy and quaint. The menu is New Florida cuisine with entrees ranging from cornmeal crusted tournedos of beef with Dijon mustard sauce to speckled trout with ginger and coconut milk. Old City House's Sunday brunch is definitely a special treat. The recipes that follow were provided by Sous Chef Roger Millecan.

MIXED GREENS WITH CITRUS

Romaine lettuce
red leaf lettuce
bibb lettuce
endive

orange, peeled
pineapple, sliced
Honey Dressing (recipe
follows)

Wash the greens. Arrange on a plate with peeled orange and pineapple sections. Top with honey dressing.

Honey Dressing
2 tablespoons sugar
1 teaspoon paprika
1 teaspoon dry mustard
1/4 teaspoon black pepper

1/4 cup lemon juice
3/4 cup salad oil
1/3 cup honey
1 teaspoon celery seed

Combine all ingredients and whisk until mixed thoroughly. Then chill before serving.

SEVEN HERB FRIED EGGS

1 teaspoon salt
1 teaspoon white pepper
1 teaspoon sage
1 teaspoon thyme

1 teaspoon basil
1 teaspoon paprika
1 teaspoon garlic powder
eggs

Combine the herbs and sprinkle on eggs. Cook the eggs to your preference.

Spinach Salad

spinach, washed
mushrooms, sliced
blue cheese

sesame seeds
ground pepper to taste
roasted garlic vinaigrette
(recipe follows)

Wash and de-stem spinach. Drain and arrange on plates. Top with sliced mushrooms, blue cheese, sesame seeds and ground pepper. Pour on the roasted garlic vinaigrette.

Roasted Garlic Vinaigrette
3 garlic bulbs
2 teaspoons Dijon mustard
1/4 cup red wine vinegar

1/4 cup balsamic vinegar
1 1/2 cups olive oil
1/2 teaspoon salt
1 teaspoon honey

Slice off tops of garlic bulbs. Cover with olive oil and roast at 400° for 45 minutes. Remove the skin. Mix garlic and other ingredients except oil in food processors until smooth. Slowly add oil to emulsify.

Baked Garlic and Cheese Grits

1 teaspoon salt
2 1/2 teaspoons minced garlic
8 cups water
2 cups hominy grits
1 cup sweet butter

2 cups heavy cream
8 eggs, beaten
1 cup sharp Cheddar,
   shredded
1/2 teaspoon cayenne pepper

Bring water and salt to a boil. Slowly stir in grits, cover and simmer for one hour, stirring occasionally. Remove from heat. Stir in butter, garlic, cayenne and cream. Let cool. Beat in eggs and half the cheese. Fill two two-quart casseroles. Bake at 350° for one hour. Sprinkle remaining cheddar on top 15 minutes before the dish is done.

Yield: two two-quart casseroles.

ASPARAGUS WITH CASHEW BUTTER

3 pounds fresh asparagus
1/2 cup sweet butter
5 teaspoons lemon juice

1/2 teaspoon dried marjoram
3/4 cup salted cashews,
  coarsely chopped

Cook asparagus in salted water until tender, about 15 minutes. Drain. Melt butter in a sauce pan. Add lemon juice, marjoram and cashews. Simmer five minutes and pour over cooked asparagus.

FILET MEDALLIONS

beef tenderloin
1 tablespoon olive oil
salt and pepper, to taste
English muffin

poached egg
blanched asparagus tips
Cream Cheese Hollandaise
  (recipe follows)

Clean a beef tenderloin of fat and silverskin. Slice into two ounce portions. Prepare the hollandaise. Heat olive oil in a sauce pan to a very high temperature. Sprinkle medallions with salt and pepper and sear each side for about one minute. Transfer to a toasted English muffin, top with a poached egg and blanched asparagus tips. Finish with a cream cheese Hollandaise sauce.

Cream Cheese Hollandaise
2 8-ounce packages cream
  cheese
4 eggs

4 tablespoons fresh squeezed
  lemon juice
1/2 teaspoon salt

Add the eggs one at a time to the cream cheese, blending well after each addition. Add lemon juice and salt. Heat over double boiler, stirring until thick and fluffy.

This Atlantic Beach restaurant is the destination for good food and fun. Its location cannot be beat; where Atlantic Boulevard meets the ocean. The setting is rustic with beautiful carved wood, bricks and lots of greenery. Ragtime is known for its Cajun-inspired seafood and fresh key lime cheesecake. Home-brewed beer is served up in the Tap Room. Ragtime is owned by the Morton brothers. Chef Tim Sizer provided the Ragtime recipes. The Mortons and Chef Sizer have just opened another very promising restaurant. A1A Ale Works is located in the heart of historic St. Augustine. This new restaurant features a brewery and New World cuisine.

*R*ED BEANS AND RICE

1 quart red beans	1 tablespoon thyme
1 cup chopped yellow onion	1 tablespoon black pepper
1 cup chopped green onion	1 teaspoon cayenne
1 cup chopped green pepper	5 bay leaves
1/2 cup chopped celery	1 tablespoon basil
4 ounces liquid smoke flavoring	1 tablespoon onion powder
4 ounces garlic, minced	1 teaspoon red pepper flakes
2 ounces salt	1 quart cooked warm white rice

Soak the beans for 24 hours with water two inches above the beans. Drain the water, then add enough water to cover the beans plus two inches. Add all the other ingredients, except the rice. Simmer for one hour or until tender, adding water if needed. (Bean au jus should be of gravy consistency.) Place warm rice on serving plate, smother with red beans and garnish with sliced green onion.

Serves: 12.

CRAWFISH ETOUFFEE

3 cups basic white rice, uncooked
3 teaspoons salt
3 teaspoons cayenne pepper
1 teaspoon white pepper
2 teaspoons basil
2 teaspoons thyme
1/2 cup chopped red pepper
1/4 cup chopped celery
1/4 cup chopped green pepper

2 pounds cooked crawfish tails
4 cups seafood stock (base can be found in grocery stores)
1/4 cup chopped yellow onion
6 ounces flour
6 ounces peanut oil
1 cup chopped green onions
8 ounces solid butter

In a cast iron skillet, heat oil and flour. Stir until roux turns red (approximately 15 minutes). Be careful - it's hot. Add the celery, green pepper, red pepper and yellow onion. Cook until translucent. Add the seafood stock and all the seasonings. Simmer for 10 minutes. Add the crawfish and scallion. Cook for three minutes. Add the butter and continue stirring until butter is dissolved. Serve over hot rice immediately. Garnish with the green onions.

Serves: 12.

GUMBO

2 ounces olive oil
2 ounces fresh minced garlic
2 cups medium diced onion
1 cup medium diced green bell pepper
1/2 cup finely sliced green onion
3 cups fresh diced tomato
2 cups frozen cut okra
1 teaspoon liquid smoke flavoring

3 bay leaves, whole
1 teaspoon thyme
1 ounce salt
1 tablespoon cayenne pepper
8 allspice berries
1/2 teaspoon ground mace
1/2 teaspoon ground clove
4 ounces white wine
2 cups water
4 ounces brown or red roux (see note)

Heat oil in pot. When the oil begins to lightly smoke, add garlic. Cook for 30 seconds and add vegetables. When the onions are translucent, add all of the remaining ingredients and bring to a light simmer. Simmer for one hour.

Note: Roux is a mixture of 50% butter and 50% flour. To get a dark color from the roux, put equal amounts of flour and butter in a saute´pan over medium high heat, whisking constantly until it turns a reddish color (approximately 20 minutes for one cup of roux). Be extremely careful when attempting this, the mixture will get to over 500 degrees. Be careful!

One or any of the following may be added: Andouille cured/smoked sausage, taso-cured ham, cooked chicken meat, blue crab claws (cooked), cooked shrimp or cooked crawfish tail meat.

Serves: 12.

 ## VOODOO SHRIMP AND CRAWFISH

10 pounds live crawfish	4 lemons, cut into quarters
4 pounds 31-35 count fresh shrimp	6 jalapeno peppers, cut in half (seeds and all)
6 ears corn, cut into thirds	1 ounce whole allspice berries
4 pounds small red potatoes	1 ounce whole cloves
1 1/2 pounds crawfish boil (purchase at seafood market)	8 dashes hot pepper sauce
	6 bottles Dixie beer
salt, to taste	6 gallons water

Combine all the ingredients except the seafood and bring to a boil. When the potatoes and corn are tender, add the seafood and cook for eight minutes or until the shrimp are firm and the crawfish are bright red. Drain and serve with drawn butter and cocktail sauce.

Serves: 12.

River City Brewing Co. is a huge, bustling microbrewery located right on the St. Johns River. This modern wood and glass restaurant has spectacular views of downtown Jacksonville. It has been fascinating to watch this place. Jim and Jeff Lee, two successful Boston restaurateurs, took over the property and lured celebrity Chefs, Tim and Barbara Felver. River City's menu is eclectic with selections such as coconut shrimp, pan-fried bean cakes, seafood jambalaya, prime rib, Cuban pasta, pan-seared local flounder, creme brulee and profiteroles (French puff pastry stuffed with vanilla ice cream and served with chocolate sauce).

BLACK BEAN CAKE

1 pound black beans
3 thick strips bacon, diced
1 carrot, diced
1 onion, diced
9 cloves garlic, ground
1/2 bunch thyme
2 teaspoons cumin
1 chipolte

1 ham hock
chicken stock, add 1 to 1 with
 water to cover beans
2 red peppers, diced
2 yellow peppers, diced
3 pablano peppers, diced
1 onion, diced
1 tablespoon garlic, ground

Heat heavy sauce pot. Sauté bacon, carrots, diced onion, garlic and thyme. Add the beans, water, stock, chipolte, cumin and ham hock. Bring to a boil, reduce heat to simmer. Cook covered until soft. When cooked strain through chinacap saving the cooking liquid. Rough chop beans in robo-coup then place in a bowl. Mix in liquid until it forms a ball. Heat a pan with margarine then saute onions, garlic, red, yellow and pablano peppers. Pour off oil and add to beans. Form eight ounce patties and store on sheet pans separating the layers with parchment paper. When ready to serve, pan saute and top with salsa.

Sterling's Cafe is an elegant bistro located in the heart of historic Avondale. The atmosphere is light and airy. The cafe is known for dishes with an innovative flair. Chef Gillian Smith offers a diverse menu from the ethnic to the traditional. Potato-crusted grouper, Veal Sterling's and Pasta Milano are among the most popular entrees. Frank Gallo, who owns and manages Sterling's, started there as a waiter. Word has it that he still tries his hand at waiting tables, occasionally.

ENGLISH CUSTARD TART

Paté Sucreé
3/4 cup flour
pinch salt
1/4 cup super fine sugar

4 tablespoons butter
2 egg yolks
1 tablespoon cornmeal
filling (recipe follows)

Sift flour and salt together on a work surface. Make a well in the center and add egg yolks, sugar and butter. Pinch and work them together, gradually working in all the flour. Add a few drops of ice water, if needed, to work in all the flour. Knead until smooth, wrap in plastic wrap and refrigerate one hour. Roll out on a little flour mixed with cornmeal. Place cornmeal side down in a 9-inch pie pan, trim and flute edges. Prick the bottom of the pie crust with a fork, line with parchment paper and a few beans as pie weights to prevent rising. Bake five to 10 minutes at 325°, or until barely golden. Prepare the filling. Strain the filling through a sieve and pour into prepared shell. Grate fresh nutmeg generously over top and bake in 350° oven for 20 to 25 minutes, until soft set. Pie should jiggle slightly. Serve warm, room temperature or chilled with fresh raspberries or strawberries.

Hint: Add one teaspoon of grated lemon rind for a lovely fresh lemon flavor.

Filling
1 pint heavy cream
3 eggs

1/2 teaspoon vanilla
whole nutmeg
1/2 cup sugar

Place the eggs, cream, sugar and vanilla in a medium mixing bowl. Mix with a wire whip until well incorporated.

West River is located in Avondale at the end of a circa-1950 retail establishment adjacent to an overpass. Walls are pastel with white architectural details. Muted paintings and lush piano music enhance the warm, classical ambience. The menu features contemporary American cuisine, fish, pasta and Caribbean-style dishes. Liz Grenamyer is the Executive Chef.

*M*EDITERRANEAN SALAD

1 plum tomato, cut into eighths
6 mushrooms, halved
1/3 zucchini, sliced in half lengthwise, then sliced into disks
1/4 eggplant, chopped into cubes
1/2 carrot, sliced thin
2-3 broccoli florets
6 basil leaves, chopped
1 sprig rosemary, chopped
1 teaspoon salt
2 tablespoons olive oil
1/2 teaspoon lemon juice

1/2 teaspoon balsamic vinegar
pinch cracked pepper
1 cup mixed greens
1 tablespoon flour (for dredging)
2 tablespoons olive oil (for sauteing)
1/4 cup bread crumbs
1 ounce Parmesan cheese, grated
2 ounces goat cheese, cut into rounds
1 egg, beaten

Preheat oven to 350°. Toss vegetables in oil, lemon juice and vinegar. Roast on sheet pan for 15-20 minutes, until just cooked. Be careful not to burn broccoli. Transfer to a mixing bowl and toss with basil, rosemary and salt. Set aside. Dredge the goat cheese rounds in salt and pepper seasoned flour. Dip in beaten egg and allow excess to drip off. Dredge in bread crumbs and Parmesan cheese. Saute´ in olive oil until golden, turn and saute other side until golden. Place greens on salad plate. Arrange the roasted vegetables over the greens. Decorate with sauteed goat cheese rounds on top.

The Wine Cellar, a veritable grande dame of the Jacksonville restaurant scene, celebrated its 20th anniversary in 1994. The Wine Cellar is located across from the historic Treaty Oak on Jacksonville's Southbank. The restaurant's interior features light walls, wood panels and fascinating walls of wine corks which makes for a charming, soothing atmosphere. There is also a brick paved patio graced by an overhead grape arbor for outside dining. The Wine Cellar is known for its excellent Continental fare: grilled Norwegian salmon, Steak Diane, Grecian shrimp and rack of lamb. It is no surprise that this restaurant features an impressive wine list. Debra Hines is the Chef and Vicki Dugan owns the Wine Cellar.

GRECIAN SHRIMP AND SCALLOPS

10 shrimp
10 scallops
3 teaspoons lemon juice
3 teaspoons butter
1 small garlic clove, minced
1/3 cup chopped green
   onions

1 large tomato, cut into
   wedges
1/3 teaspoon oregano
2 teaspoons sliced black olives
salt and white pepper, to taste
1/3 pound feta cheese, cubed
1/4 cup cream sherry

Sprinkle the shrimp and scallops with lemon juice and set aside. Melt butter in large skillet. Saute´ the garlic, green onion and tomato wedges. Add the shrimp and scallops and season with oregano, salt and pepper to taste. Turn the shrimp frequently and saute until pink. Add the feta cheese, black olives and cream sherry. Bring to a boil and cook for three to four minutes. Serve over fettucine.

Serves: two.

CONTRIBUTORS

Many thanks to all of those who contributed information for this book. We could not have done it without you!

Barbara Burt Allen
Tracey Austin
Donna Bailey
Sue Bailey
Sherri Barnes
Donna Bateh
Carol Baumer
Deb Burdeshaw Becker
Lisa Benton
Lynda Bryant
Violet Cadorette
Shan Caffey
Gowie Cassell
Olita Cerni
Diane Claiborne
Winslow Colbert
Linea Collecelli
Julie Cook
Nancy Coxen
Sissy Crabtree
Jill Dame
Catherine Purcell Damron
Amy Conger Davenport
Eloise Conger Davenport
Gay Dawson
Carol Dent
Patty DeStephano
Margaret Eggleston
Ann Engelhardt
Saskia Etheridge
Chef Dean Fearing
Ann Gibbs
Elaine Conger Gist

Velma Graham Gist
Monteen Gnann
Allison Greenwood
Deborah Griffin
Georgann Harben
Pat Harris
Anne Phillips Hartje
Chris Hayes
Anita L. Hemrick
Anne Hepler
Debi Hilaman
Vera F. Hitchcock
Marianne Hofheimer
Jeri Hogan
Margi Hogan
Leigh Holman
Brucie Hooper
Margaret Ann Howell
Frances Hudson
Judy Hughs
Kim Joel
Dorothy Johnson
Isabell Johnson
Lori Joyce
Shelley Klempf
Laura J. Klempf
Patti Moore LaForce
Gay Gamble Landaiche
Beth Langley
Camille McEachern Leifeste
Lee Anne MacDade
Barbara Hutchison Magee
Suzanne Wagner Magee

Mary Matta
Elise Maynard
Elna Mays
Kathryn McCamy
Catherine McCullough
Gene McDaniel
Elise Fernandez McKeever
Eileen McVeigh
Mary Meagher
Kenyon Varn Merritt
Jeanne Mileur
Max Mileur
Susan Mitdol
Rebecca Bray Monroe
Suzanne Morris
Martha Fry Morrow
Kristin Nell Mosely
Jenny Mottier
Sherrill Mullens
Joanelle Mulrain
Abby Myers
Martha Nicolini
Loretta Nido
Lizzie Oliphint
Frances Palmer
Kay Park
Jean Parks
Cindy Patterson
Paula Phelan
Amy Elizabeth Pritchett
Leslie Ralph
Genevieve Reddick
Lisa Reel
Leslie M. Reid

Julie F. Rice
Susan Ring
Sally Robbins
Frances Rodriguez
Mimi R. Rosen
Debbie Rouse
Jane Anders Ruffin
Susan Saunders
Becky Schatz
Libby Schaller
Joann Marie Schellenberg
Elizabeth Sharpe
Katherine Godfrey Skinner
Lacey Skinner
Virgina Brightman Skinner
Leslie Skipper
Susan Snelson
Sandy Sntonopoulos
Randy Stephens
Susan Thedford
Martha M. Thompson
Marilyn Thornton
Carol Triano
Linda Tyre
Dana Lee Walker
Zolina Walker
Bev Warren
Kathy Wedbush
Sharon Wilkinson
Molly Williams
Martha L. Womack
Sharon Dengel Wulbern
Phillipa Yant

$\mathscr{I}$NDEX

A River Runs Backward
Order Form

A River Runs Backward
The Junior League of Jacksonville
2165 Park Street
Jacksonville, Florida 32204

Please send_____copies of *A River Runs Backward* @ $19.95 each $_____
Postage and handling (in the continental U.S.)   @ $3.50 each $_____
Florida residents add 6.5% sales tax each book   @ $1.30 each $_____
                                                                TOTAL $_____

Name _____

Address _____

City_____State _____Zip _____

Make checks payable to:

THE JUNIOR LEAGUE OF JACKSONVILLE, FLORIDA, INC.

For further information please call (904) 387-9927 or FAX (904) 387-5497

A River Runs Backward
Order Form

A River Runs Backward
The Junior League of Jacksonville
2165 Park Street
Jacksonville, Florida 32204

Please send_____copies of *A River Runs Backward* @ $19.95 each $_____
Postage and handling (in the continental U.S.)   @ $3.50 each $_____
Florida residents add 6.5% sales tax each book   @ $1.30 each $_____
                                                                TOTAL $_____

Name _____

Address _____

City_____State _____Zip _____

Make checks payable to:

THE JUNIOR LEAGUE OF JACKSONVILLE, FLORIDA, INC.

For further information please call (904) 387-9927 or FAX (904) 387-5497

If you would like to see

A RIVER RUNS BACKWARD

in your area, please send the name and
address of your local gift or book stores.

Thank you for your support!

THE JUNIOR LEAGUE OF JACKSONVILLE, FLORIDA

If you would like to see

A RIVER RUNS BACKWARD

in your area, please send the name and
address of your local gift or book stores.

Thank you for your support!

THE JUNIOR LEAGUE OF JACKSONVILLE, FLORIDA